THE ESCAPED HORSE

COLLECTED FANZINES

Mark Staniforth (ed.)

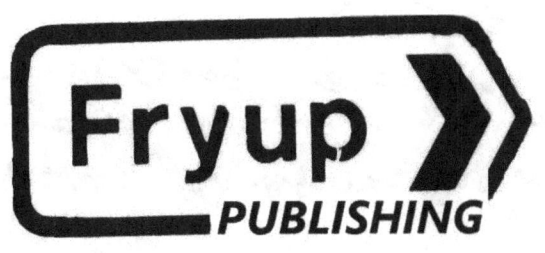
Fryup PUBLISHING

ISBN 978-0-244-95095-8
90000

It is a well-known historical fact that Friedrich Nietzsche established one of his most enduring philosophical theories after watching Thornton-le-Dale Football Club thump and grind their way to a goalless draw in the bowels of Scarborough and District League Division Three. "In individuals, insanity is rare," proposed Nietzsche, "but in groups.. it is the rule." Nietzsche nailed it. At the sound of the referee's whistle, normally mild-mannered men would turn borderline psychopathic; monosyllabic fools could be heard spewing extraordinary feats of syntactical parallelism; octogenarian spectators invoked the spirit of Muhammad Ali by wading onto the playing field to swing their fists at opponents less than one quarter their age. 'The Escaped Horse' was hunched on the touchline to chronicle it all. In its two short years in existence, it was variously lauded as "a load of fucking bollocks", "a complete waste of fucking money", and "a fucking liberty". Its editors were routinely verbally abused, and occasionally physically threatened. There was an official move by the league itself to issue them with banning orders. Undeterred, 'The Escaped Horse' continued to scoop the dregs from the village pub's empty pint glasses and finger grubby Friday night ash-trays in order to unearth the sordid truth about its urine and black-shirted heroes. Riding the wave of the early 1990s football fanzine craze, its heady blend of prurience and puerility became essential reading for those who feared their drunken antics or sexual misdemeanours might somehow find their way to being published for posterity. This re-print of the entire back-catalogue is intended to acknowledge that such fears were not misplaced. But also, in today's Sky TV era of corporate-

-endorsed millionaire superstars, it aims to act as a timely reminder of what the sport at its arse-end is really all about. Some of its heroes have since passed on: to each of them we owe genuine gratitude for colouring our late-childhoods with laughter, and teaching us words for parts of the female anatomy that we never knew existed, and more than two decades on have still not managed to find. To all those other living, breathing, potential litigants out there, we simply say this: we hope you accept this re-production in the nostalgia-soaked spirit in which it is intended. We seldom re-visit Thornton-le-Dale today, largely through fear of brooding vendettas. The legendary Greyhound Ground is long gone; an all-mod-cons new complex nearer the village centre speaking volumes for the club's new-found air of professionalism. Frankly, we preferred the mucky old days: the days when the goalkeeper stubbing his fag out before kick-off could be a cause for outrageous optimism. 'The Escaped Horse' petered out after fifteen-and-a-bit editions and a couple of specials, its editors having come to the belated conclusion that there were better ways to spend our Saturday afternoons than incessantly barracking a bunch of hapless neanderthals. We left with the rant of one last visiting goalkeeper - "Shut your fucking gobs and fuck off!" ringing in our ears, and the lyrics from our favourite mid-match chant emblazoned upon our hearts for ever more:

We're hot-shot Thornton
We are the super Dale
Everybody knows our ground is up for sale
No times we've won the Cup
And number nought is coming up
We're hot-shot Thornton Dale

"I fair clogged 'im one"
— Deggy Bond

A THORNTON DALE FC FANZINE   SCARBOROUGH LEAGUE DIV. 3 1990/1

NOT BAD FOR ONLY 15p!   ISSUE 1

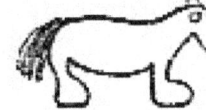

THE ESCAPED HORSE

****

So, a new season is upon us once again, and Dale are chasing that
illustrious 3rd place spot for the 4th year in succession. Dale have
already started their season with a home game against Beckett League
Gillamoor which ended in a 1-1 draw. One amazing story from this match
was that Eddie 'Slap' Avison was heard to apologise to an opponent after
he had deliberately chopped him!

****

During the forthcoming season, the following groans and grumbles will
probably be heard around the ground:

STEVE AVISON: F*** OFF!

EDDIE AVISON: SHUT UP, OUR KID!

ANDY HILL: HOW MANY ARE LEEDS LOSING BY!

VICTOR WELBURN: NOT TODAY, I'VE RETIRED!

BRIAN BEST: OH, YOU'RE CRAP, YOU LOT!

****

PLAYER'S NICKNAMES - PART 1

WHY IS ANDY HILL CALLED 'SNEBBER'?   EXCLUSIVE FEATURE...

Andy Hill works in a very competitive job market, the trusty apprentice of
Ralphie the window cleaner. The partnership
can be spotted easily every day of the week,
as Snebber usually wears a T-Shirt with
the name of an unknown pop group sprawled
across it, and Ralph's pride and joy is a
Leeds United 'shit or bust' shirt.
But why is Andy Hill called Snebber? Is 'sneb'
a medieval word for nose? Or is the word
associated with stupid hair styles?
If Andy Hill wants us to stop calling him
this fascinating name, we give him this
plea from the bottom of our hearts...
GET YOUR HAIR CUT!

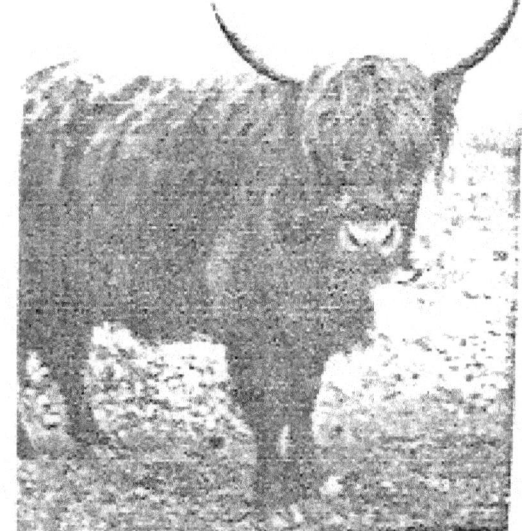

SNEBBER IN THE SCOTTISH HIGHLANDS

As this recent photo shows,
he is still not complying
with our wishes!

££

DEDICATED TO:
                                        £
                                        £
George Ripley, referee extrodinaire £
and the downfall of Mermaid FC   £
                                        £

A THORNTON DALE FC FANZINE   SCARBORO LEAGUE DIV 3

*** £1 LESS THAN 'FOOTBALL MONTHLY' * * * ISSUE 2

THE escaped Horse

****

We start this edition with news that issue 1 of this fantastic
fanzine was a complete sell-out! Good news for Andy Hill. On the
subject of Andy Hill, the reason why there is not much Snebber
slagging in this issue has absolutely nothing to do with the fact
that he was blubbering and crying and giving us physical and verbal
abuse after he read edition 1, the truth is that we are saving
up information and pictures for an Andy Hill special to be
released later in the season...Bet you can't wait, Sneb!

****

BRIAN BEST - THE FACTS...

When Besty left us he probably thought that we would not have a
decent striker any more and we would plummet to the bottom of
division 3, but how wrong he is. Star signing Shaun Dixon came
straight into the side and slammed in a hat-rick. When was the
last time Besty got 3 goals in 1 match? And we will end this
tribute with Besty's famous saying, which no doubt he will be
yelling at his Wykeham team-mates shortly...
              'OH, YOU'RE CRAP, YOU LOT'

****

THANKS TO:

Lineker and Howell for
scoring against Leeds
last saturday,Shaun
Dixon for scoring
against Brompton,Victor
for giving us his very
deep half time views at
Brompton,new star signing
Julian Bevan for giving
us an exculsive interview
and of course the escaped
horse.

NO THANKS TO:

Andy Hill,Julian Bevan
for giving us a crap
interview,and MERMAID FC

****

DEDICATED TO:

Anyone who has bought
this excellent fanzine
and again to the downfall
of Mermaid F.C
****

W 4 PAGES !!!

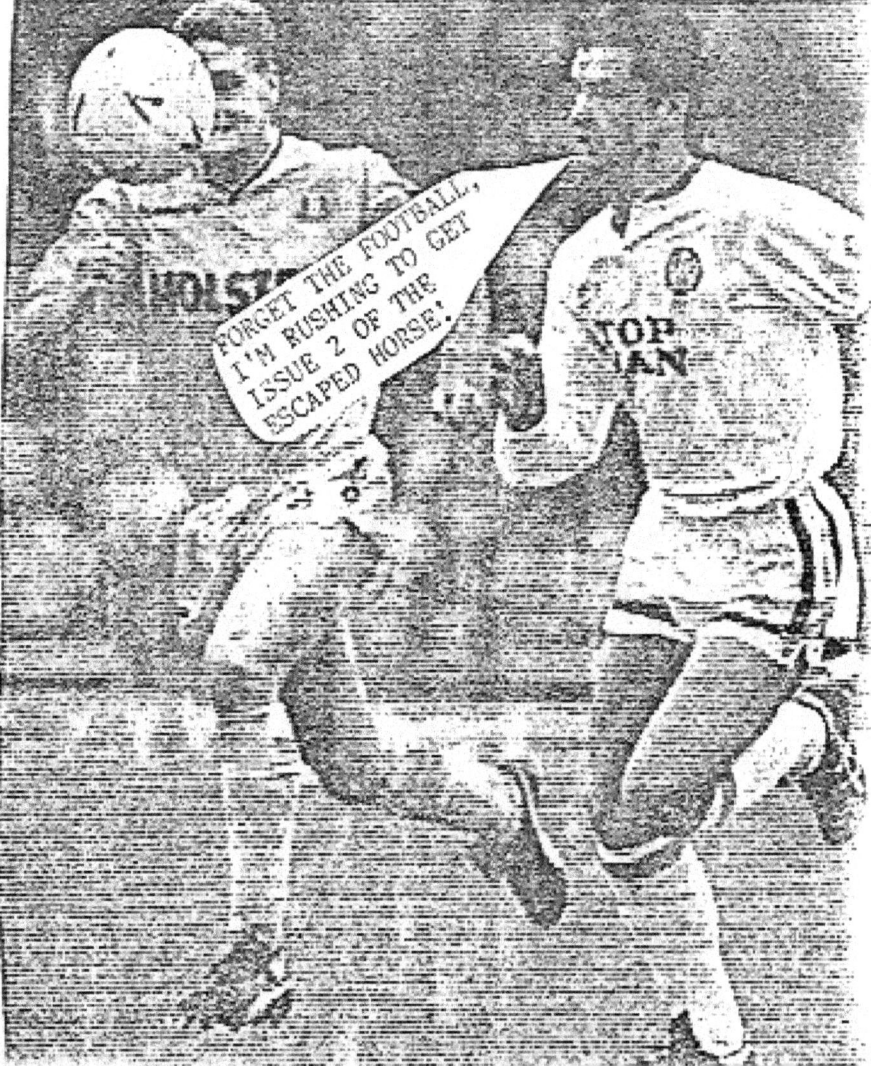

FORGET THE FOOTBALL, I'M RUSHING TO GET ISSUE 2 OF THE ESCAPED HORSE!

THE ENTIRE HISTORY OF MERMAID F.C

MATCH REPORT-THORNTON DALE v BROMPTON

FIRST HALF:

After just ten minutes of what Mick Barnes described to be a hard match before the game, Brompton took the lead. Mick Barnes failed to clear a simple lob through the middle, as Mike Aconley called it, and a mop of white hair easily lobbed Stuart Hill in the Thornton goal. This for some obscure reason sent this Wurzel Gumage into fits of ecstasy while others just stood and watched. We would just like to say to Wurzel how much of a prick he really did look.

But not all was lost as nine minutes later Richard Bradley pinpointed an excellent cross (yes Richard Bradley!) to the far post where Shaun Dixon was waiting to neatly head the ball home, a bloody good goal. One all.

Seconds later Will Balderson hit the bar at his own end from a Brompton corner. Pretty nerveracking stuff. One one it stayed till half time with both sides using substitute. Mark Bagnel came on for a limping Billy Atkinson.

Mike Aconley didn't comment at half time so Victor did the honours, "could 'ave done better". Thanks Victor very intellectual!.

SECOND HALF:

Three minutes into the second half and the capacity crowd witnessed another great goal. Shaun Dixon again was put through from a long a long ball from the halfway line to score another excellent goal. Seven minutes later on and guess who was sent through to head past the keeper. Yes our star player Shaun Dixon. Why hasn't he being playing for longer? It may have been an own goal but it was good enough for us.

A minute later and the last chance probably for Brompton as Mick Barnes attempted to get them back in the game by heading past his own keeper, but he was foiled by the skills of Stuart Hill.

The only booking was for Will Balderson after seventy minutes for a miniscule incident (bit harder next time Will, it makes good reading).

After match comments from the management were as follows; Mick Barnes- "I'm Knackered", Mike Aconley- "great highlight front running duo Bradley and Dixon. Six out of ten, it was an average game.

Well 3-1 over Brompton isn't too bad at all. It was a good entertaining game getting better towards the second half. But what happened to the defence. Yes you Mick Barnes, it wasn't exactly a fabulous performance now was it? But all in all can't complain it was a good result.

We would also like to say Brian Best can stay where he is, Shaun Dixon is bloody amazing and miles better than you anyway!
****
Also there would be a report on the 2-0 thrashing of Hummanby but we cant remember bugger all about that game so all you get is what we can scrabble our brains for. Good goals were scored by Bradley and Shepherd but Rich should have scored a lot more.
****

THE ESCAPED HORSE POEM. VOL 1 NO 1.

In the first round We made such a sound Snebber could not fail As we thrashed Ryedale	GREAT GROUNDS
	GANTON;
We met Wykeham in round two And Besty we did boo Andy Hill scored seven And we were in heaven	CHANGING ROOMS - Luxury and spacious caravan with plenty of air ventilation!
In the quarters we met Fishburn Park And Sneb again was on the mark We tore apart the Whitby side As Andy took them for a ride	PITCH - Great slant, massive mole hills and bugger all in the way of goal nets!
In the semis we scaled the dizzy heights And Snebber again disposed of Sleights His crosses were brilliant, the box he did raid We were into the final, against Mermaid	PROGRAMME PRICE - No known issue for last season's game! GROUND CAPACITY - God knows how many!
In the last minute, the score sat one all And Rich Bradley was on the ball As his cross came over, Snebber rose And the ball went in right off his NOSE!	NUMBER OF SEATS - 4 in Mike's car! TOILETS - Nearest hedge only a short walk away.
And you thought it was a slag free issue Sneb! *********************************	OTHER NOTES - Force 10 wind, useless team and an over - whelming smell of pig shite!

EIGHT THINGS THE MERMAID MANAGER MAY HAVE SAID (AND THEIR MEANINGS)

1. I can't see myself ever leaving this club.
   (I have no ambition whatsoever.)
2. We are not just a one-man team.
   (One day, someone other than gooseneck will actually score a goal.)
3. Anything can happen in the cup.
   (Please God not them Thornton yobs again.)
4. It's early days yet.
   (We have only won once in our first twelve games.)
5. You need a bit of luck in this game.
   (All our goals were offside.)
6. In our last game we lacked in vocal support.
   (There were twice as many visiting supporters.)
7. Our discipline problem is getting better.
   (We are down to an average of two sendings off per game.)
8. Not our most encouraging performance of the season.
   (As usual we were BOLLOCKS.)
****

QUOTE OF THE WEEK

RALPH SPEAKING ABOUT ANDY HILL

"HIS NOSE ISN'T BIG, IT JUST GROWS WHEN HE LIES!"
(yes folks, he really DID say that!!!)

THE ESCAPED HORSE

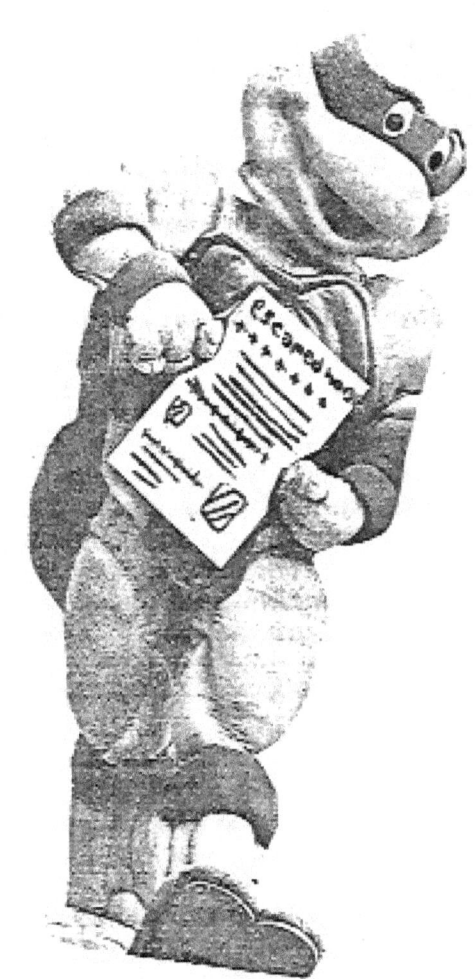

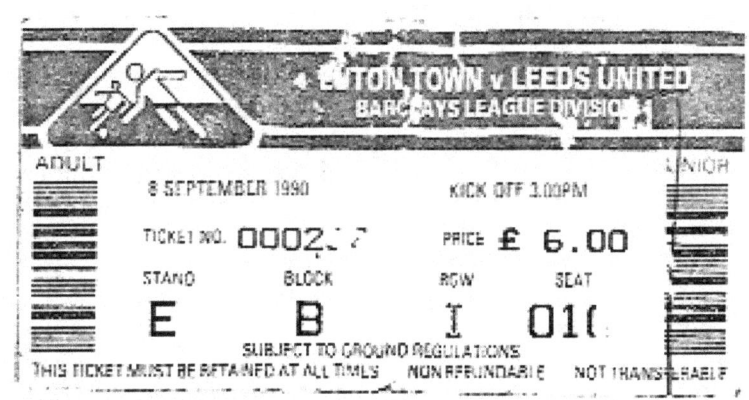

WHO'S BEEN A
NAUGHTY BOY THEN,
RALPHIE?
AWAY FANS AT
LUTON ?!!? PAGE 2

EVEN THE
TURTLES CAN'T
RESIST THIS
WEEK'S ISSUE...

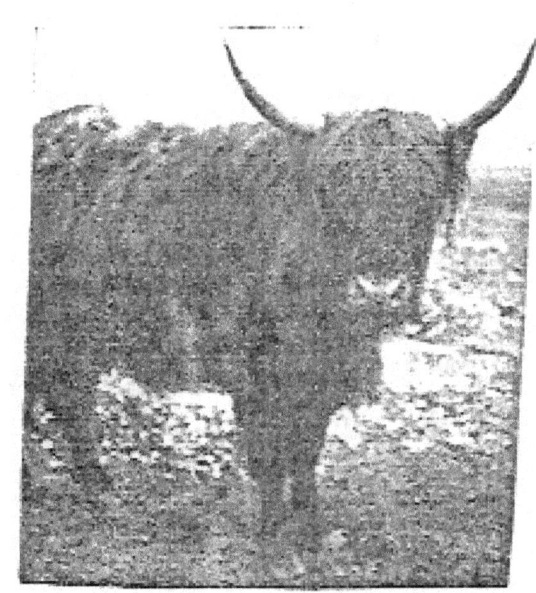

SNEBBER RETURNS

ON PAGE 2

EDITORIAL

Hello again, Dale fans, and we again start this issue with news that number 2 of the 'ESCAPED HORSE' was a complete and utter sell-out! Therefore you cannot buy it again unless you offer us a couple of quid to cover printing costs, VAT etc. Not too much Snebber slagging this issue as he's getting too much publicity but the occasional word won't go amiss! Also we would like to say that we were up till God knows when last night finishing off this fantastic fanzine, so keep the money rolling in, remember all proceeds go to the club at the end of the season. Oh and in case you were wondering who that long haired hippy was last weekend, we reveal all the secrets, just read on...

****

THE LEGEND IS BACK

Yes, the man himself is back. After the recent defeat at Barrowcliff, Snebber said he had 'had enough of this shit' and would be back at Christmas. Well, Christmas must have come early this year, there he was last week banging in a goal for the Dale. We were so amazed that Snebber had the courage to appear in front of the Dales roaring fans that we completely forgot to slag him off! Anyway, as a tribute to this 'golden great' we have printed his photo again on the cover.
As you can see, it is just the same Andy Hill as before, hair pointing promenent like Wigan pier and his locks blowing behind him in the wind. Here at the Escaped Horse, we would like to wish him all the best for his new career, start hitting the net, get yer hair cut, and keep your hands off them Ozzie lassies, eh?!?

****

LEEDS FAN GETS IN AT LUTON!

Yep, unfortuneately it's true, Ralphie just won't give up, he just has to get to every home and away game (God knows why) and only Ralphie would go all the way to Luton and manage to nick a ticket from somewhere to get in. The ticket shown on the cover was found by your roving reporters somewhere in the vicinity of Ralph's dwelling, we know it must be his, as who else supports L**ds United? Hopefully next issue we will be able to tell you how he actually got hold of this ticket. Tut tut Ralphie!

****

BRIAN BEST EXCLUSIVE

It looks like ex Thornton Dale star winger is going downhill! A little birdy told us at the last home game (no names mentioned to protect the innocent) that BB had been dropped from the second division Wykeham side. Looks like we were right after all, Shaun Dixon is a lot better and you can stay wheree you are. Hopefully an exclusive interview with Brian Best for a later issue but no promises at this stage.

****

THANKS TO	NO THANKS TO
Mick Barnes for lending us the paper for the last match report	The Northcliff keeper for giving us shit last week.
Andy Hill for giving us someone to shout at on Saturday	The ref last week for moving us from our usual spot behind the goal.
The Turtle for posing for us on the cover	Mermaid FC as usual.
ALL OF YOU WHO BOUGHT THIS RAG KEEP THE MONEY FLOODING IN!	If he hasn't bought this fanzine and is reading yours, Andy Hill!

MATCH REPORTS   THIS WEEK - 2 FOR THE PRICE OF 1!!!!!!

BARROWCLIFF AWAY

Barrowcliff won every game last year so we knew we'd get pissed on
even before we went to Scarborough, sure enough, Barrowcliff had gone
ahead after only 2 minutes. Dale still had time to get back into the
game, but a sudden cry of "Oh Shit!" from the Dales travelling army
meant that Barrowcliff had scored again. After this terrible start
the game seemed to be settling down but just as Thornton woke up, they
scored again! We all knew what Barney would think of this at half time
but we don't want to print this in the fanzine. The Scarborough side
scored again before half time but we were used to it by then.
Suddenly near the interval Rich Bradley actually got a shot in, but as
with most 'Bradley specials', it went hideously wide.
Half Time 4-0 to Barrowcliff

Ashley Welburn's half time views: 'Yes very nice, you can see right
over the bay!'

At the start of the second half Mark Bagnel came on for an entirely
crap and knackered Mark Shepherd, and after a scramble in the area he
actually scored, we just couldn't believe it. (We still can't)
18 minutes from the end and our ageing manager Mick Barnes was brought
off and in replace on came a youthful Dean Richardson for his dream
debut in Dales' famous yellow. But 10 minutes from the end, would you
believe it, they scored again.
Full Time 5-1 to Barrowcliff

Mike Aconley's full time views: 'Thank God for the final whistle!'

NORTH CLIFF HOME

The Dale squad came out looking confident and with 2 new players in
the side a good result was in prospect. One player we don't know who
we will refer to as 'Slaphead' and a familiar face that looked
suspiciously like Andy Hill! 1 minute gone and North Cliff scored.
Even the bias editors must admit it was a good goal, but memories of
Barrowcliff came flooding back. After 15 minutes we got our first
glance of Andy Hill's hidden talents, but he kicked the ball wide.
However he made amends 5 minutes later with a sensational goal from
the edge of the area. We were a bit angry afterwards however as he did
not respond to our 'Snebber Snebber give us a wave!' shouts. 3
minutes later they scored again, real nailbiting stuff, and soon after
Eddie Avison scored but the bias ref who was undoubtedly a North Cliff
fan in disguise disallowed it. After 28 minutes they scored again
with a header from a corner, even our most hardened fans were close to
tears, but they soon dried up as Shaun Dixon scored 1 minute later,
only to flood out in bucket loads again after the shit ref disallowed
it again. A minute from half time, Stuart Hill hit the post from a
penalty.
Half time 2-1 to North Cliff

We would just now like to give the North Cliff keeper a special
Escaped Horse F**K OFF! after he kicked our ball away and called us a
bunch of 'Crazy b****rds.' Our sorrow soon turned to joy as Eddie
Avison scored with 8 minutes gone of the second hald after a goalmouth
scramble.

continued over>>>>>>>

NORTH CLIFF REPORT CONTINUED>>>

Then the ref ordered us to leave our usual spot behind the goal and we duly took up our positions in the stand from where we had great delight in chanting 'We want Bevan!' when in fact he did not want to come on! Obviously having no fans behind the goal had an adverse affect on the players and Cliff made it 3-2, but Dale recovered and with 25 minutes left Shep scored, ace goal. After this sensational equaliser, nothing much happened, in fact we all went to sleep...
Final score 3-3

Mick Barnes' full time comment: 'Missed chances, didn't get breaks but a good fight back.'
****

BEVAN - THE TRUTH

It goes with Escaped Horse tradition that if a Dale player says anything obscene or vulgar to us, we oblige by slagging him off in the fanzine.   Well, Julian Bevan that dark haired young starlet who is already the new Gazza (he cries all the time) muttered something of this sort to us recently. All was quiet when behind us he was heard to say 'Chelsea.' Obscene enough to warrant a good slagging off, don't you think?
Well, we have decided to inform you of something that happened in the game vs North Cliff. As Dale were losing 3-2, Julian was in conversation with the other young superstar, Dean Richardson. We heard him claim that he did not want to go on, as he was scared of all the large masculine objects already on the pitch. His excuse was that his legs were not hairy enough and he would feel embarrased alongside the likes of Andy Hill, Rich Bradley etc. Dean probably felt the same but he was brave enough to tell the Escaped Horse that he would go on but there was little point as they were playing well enough anyway and if he did he would be likely to miss an open goal. Such confidence.
But the point we are making to Julian is that if he scared to play why does he stay on the Dale's books? With us paying him such high wages since his recent transfer from 'Ye Olde Corner Shoppe FC' we feel he should donate some of his income to a much needed charity, ie. The Escaped Horse. Otherwise he is nothing more than a complete waste of money. (We would say the same about Dean but he would beat us all up if he read this).

****

QUOTE OF THE WEEK

STUART HILL AT BARROWCLIFF: "You can get a Mirror for that!"
(speaking about the price of the 'Escaped Horse')

****

NOTE: If you would like to be featured in this fanzine, please slag us off as soon as possible and we will write about you accordingly.

****
NEXT ISSUE: MORE NEWS AND VIEWS PLUS A WORLD EXCLUSIVE:

'SNEBBER'S OFF TO OZZIE!'

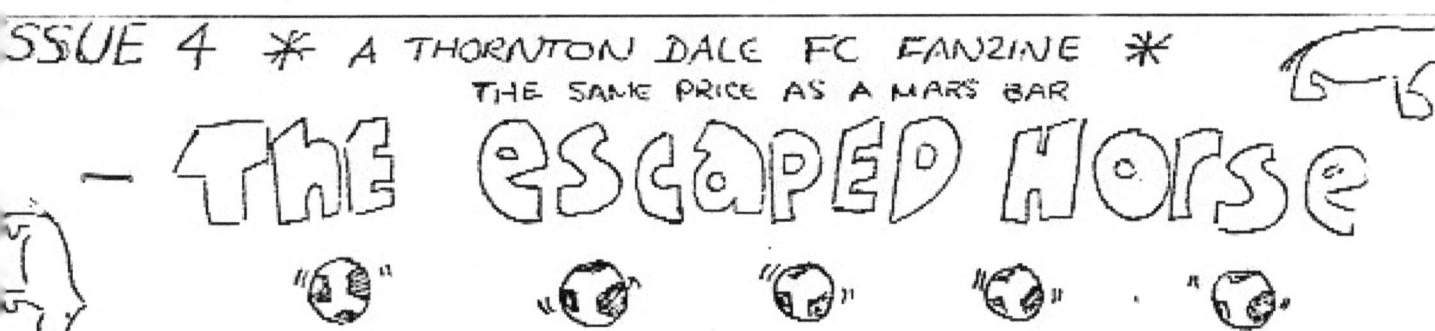

THE ESCAPED HORSE

"🐴" "🐴" "🐴" "🐴" · "🐴"

IN THE EARLY HOURS OF MONDAY, OCTOBER 15 1990, AN ENVELOPE WAS PUSHED THROUGH THE LETTERBOX AT THE 'ESCAPED HORSE' OFFICE. IT CONTAINED A SUBSTANTIAL SUM OF MONEY, AND A LETTER, WRITTEN BY THE MAN HIMSELF. IT IS REPRODUCED IN FULL, INSIDE THIS FANZINE

UNCENSORED - UNCHANGED - UNBELIEVABLE

BRIAN BEST

THE TRUTH

SENSATIONAL WORLD EXCLUSIVE

BESTY OPENS HIS

HEART TO THE HORSE

"🐴" "🐴" "🐴" "🐴" "🐴"

THE BRIAN BEST STORY

Well, here we go with the Brian Best world exclusive, written
completely by the man himself...

The Editor,
          Upon my recent visit to the Quarry Ground to watch the Dale
in action, if only to see if early season jokes were correct like
what's the difference between a triangle and the Dale? Yes, you
guessed, a triangle has three points! (Ho ho what a great sense of
humour - Eds)
   However, in general I found a poor game but there was plenty of good
work going on off the field. I was disappointed to find the money
received from the transfer of star forward Brian Best had not led to
ground improvements, however, on the bright side, I purchased a copy
of the Escaped Horse, it was nothing if not controversial. My first
thoughts were regret that such young and promising reporters had
fallen into their seniors trap, ie. if your story doesn't fit, make
it! You'll go all the way with this attitude lads!
   Touch line talk seemed to centre around player abuse, as usual,
however I have to agree I thought Steffi Graf held the record for the
largest conck - not any more - Snebber is out in front on this one,
see Carl, Mermaid FC, for cure. (Who the f**k's Carl? - bemused eds)
   One player who does take the brunt of fans backlash is young Mark
Shepherd and his weight problem. I don't agree on this one, it could
be that it's more than Mark's silky skills that will benefit the Dale,
Mark could be sold for his ivory if things stay the way they are on
the black market!!! Sorry Mark, need the money for floodlighting.
   On the Brian Best exclusive article the Dale fans should know not to
rub this star player up the wrong way as he likes nothing better than
proving rogue reporters and moles wrong, as Div 2 side Wykeham will be
at the Quarry Ground in 2 weeks time with their star, he vows to make
his feet do the talking.
   It was an enjoyable afternoon back at the Dale. I thought the game
was one of 2 halves, I drank one in the first half and one in the
second! Bye for now, keep up the good work, lads.
PS - Sorry you'll be making an early cup exit, I know the Dale need a
good cup run to keep their season alive! (BOLLOCKS!- eds)
                         yours,
                         B.Best
Leaving you with this poser - What's the difference between Ken Dodd
and the Dale? (First correct answer wins a Mars bar - QUICK SHEP!!!)
****
Besty also gave us some face to face comments during the Scalby game:
"I am a man of few words (which means he's a thick b*****d! - eds)
but I would just like to correct your statement by saying I'll be here
in 2 weeks banging in the goals. (which net? - eds) Thornton will be
going out of the SG Joiners trophy at the expense of Wykeham, but my
heart's always at Thornton. (Oh, how lovely - romantic eds)
****

QUOTES OF THE WEEK

DEAN RICHARDSON: "Shep would be a lot better if he lost 2 stone!"
SHAUN ACONLEY: "Your fanzine's crap, it doesn't have enough swearing"
(whatever will daddy say, Shaun!)
EDDIE AVISON: "Is thee simple?" (very intellectual, baldy!)
****

EDITORIAL

Well, at this rate we'll soon be into double figures, now we've reached the dizzy heights of 4 editions! Issue 3, like numbers 1 and 2 before it, was a complete sellout, if you require back issues, just give us a couple of quid and we'll see what we can do for you! Many thanks to Brian Best for his priceless contribution, wouldn't it be great if more players sent us their exclusive stories (ie. 'My nose isn't as big as Shep' by Andy Hill) Any player who does this in future will receive a free copy of the edition which features their news.
****

DEAN RICHARDSON IS A BLOODY LIAR

Yes Dean, we've heard all these allegations about you, trying to tell Shep that you didn't say "If Shep lost 2 stone he'd be a lot better". Well Shep, news for you, HE DID! And we have plenty of witnesses to prove it. Dean tried a variety of bribes etc. to stop us printing this quote, but Dean, don't think you can slag someone off at the Dale and get away with it!
****

ANDY HILL GOES TO OZZIE

Another World exclusive by the 'Escaped Horse.' We've reasons to believe that Sneb will shortly be flying out with 2 anonymous people, to begin a new life in Australia. Although turning his back on the Dale he will not be giving up football altogether but will join the quaintly named 'Kangaroo Kickers FC.' Good luck with the new career, have fun doing it upside-down, eh Andy!
****

GLEN RETURNS

Sensational news that Glen has finally returned. Big thrills.
****

JULIAN - BOLLOCKS AGAIN

Our exclusive article in Escaped Horse 3, that Julian Bevan was too scared to play for Dale, has been proved right. Last Saturday his feeble excuse was that he was sick. What will it be next time? We are already conjuring up headlines; 'BEVAN BREAKS BACK WHILE BENDING DOWN TO GIRLFRIEND NICOLE' etc etc
****

THANKS TO	NO THANKS TO
Brian Best for the exclusive writing	Wykeham FC for nicking our star player
Dean for the comment on Shep	The School holidays for making us
Shep in advance for beating Dean up	miss the Wykeham match
	Mermaid FC, naturally
Darren Acomb's biscuit tin	Darren Acomb's empty biscuit tin
And Snebber for still having the	And Mick Barnes for being himself
'largest conk.' (Quote Besty)	

****

FAMOUS DALE PLAYERS AND WHAT THEY HAVE FOR DINNER

Eddie 'your forehead dazzles us in Scarborough' Avison:
        2 mince and onion pies from Robinsons in Pickering
****
We've got some space to fill, so f**k off Andy Hill, ha ha!
****

MATCH REPORTS
SCALBY RESERVES   HOME   JUNIOR CUP ROUND 1
FIRST HALF

The first few chances in this cup game went, naturally, to the Dale.
Soon after realising their keeper was crap, a young refreshed Andy
Hill slammed in a screamer from 18 yards. Andy was on great form
(well, there's a first time for everything) and soon he would try
again, this time to be foiled by the Scalby goalie.
    The next goal came as their crap keeper fumbled the ball and Steve
Avison banged it into the net with sensational precision. (Don't know
what it means but it sounds good) By the way, a special Escaped Horse
'F**k off!' to the Scalby number 5 for calling us 'stupid c**ts.'
    But this game was soon to become as easy as jumping on a plane to
Ozzie as with 37 minutes on the clock, Snebber put away another
screamer from just inside the area. At this point the bloody rain
began to drop and it tumbled picturesquely from Andy Hill's nose.
HALF TIME: 3-0 to the Dale
HALF TIME COMMENTS: 'Excellent' - Thanks Mike!

SECOND HALF
2 minutes gone and Richard Bradley (no, it is not a misprint) scores
another from outside the area. An absolute corker!!! After 10 minutes
they actually had a shot and we were stunned, but the ever-reliable
Stuart Hill kept them at bay. At this point Andy Johnson was having a
wrestling match with his umbrella on the touchline! After this Dean
and Julian came on and what a coincidence, we didn't score any more!
(Oh and by the way Mark Shepherd was playing crap and he missed loads
of chances, YOU BIG HIPPO!
FULL TIME: 4-0 to the Dale
FULL TIME COMMENTS: 'Easy stroll' - Mike again

SCALBY   HOME   LEAGUE DIVISION 3
FIRST HALF

We were in trouble before the start of this one, as a sporty, fit
looking Mick Barnes trotted out in a yellow shirt. 5 minutes gone
though and Dale had the first chance, Shaun Dixon was put through but
of course he put it wide. Again a few minutes later Bradley was sent
through, but what do you expect from him? A good attempt this one,
though, almost knocking over the corner flag!
    After this, bugger all happened as the Dale donkeys couldn't even
get the ball into the Scalby half!

SECOND HALF
Dale started the second half with Glen Baskeyfield on the side line in
a yellow shirt. (Oh God, back to the old times again!) It is very hard
to write a report AND interview Brian Best at the same time, so
nothing much else was written. (Besides, we're running out of space)
Plenty of chances were occuring for both sides, but we just could not
get a shot in. Is this the end of Andy Hill's scoring spree? Will he
ever hit the net again? Tune in to the next edition...

FULL TIME COMMENTS: MICK BARNES: "I'm knackered" (Seem to have heard
that one before, Mick!)
MIKE ACONLEY: "Good fight, very entertaining, gritty 0-0 draw"

GOT THE ANSWER TO THE POSER ON PAGE 2 YET SHEP? THINK OF THAT MARS BAR

ISSUE 5   A THORNTON DALE FC FANZINE 1990/1

The escaped Horse

THE 'WE BASHED BESTY' EDITION

SOD OFF BESTY!

- BRADDERS BREAKS BESTY'S DREAM
- AS DYNAMIC DALE WHACK WYKEHAM

'SORRY YOU'LL BE MAKING AN EARLY CUP EXIT'

- BBest, escapedhorse no 1

ANDY HILL IS GOING BALD

- SHOCK WORLD EXCLUSIVE
(WATCH OUT EDDIE AVISON !!)
PAGE 2

PLUS + PLUS + PLUS + PLUS

* * *   MICK BARNES TELLS ALL   * * *

BEVAN GIVES HIS VIEWS ON SNEDDED'S HAIRCUT

EDITORIAL

Well here we go again, yet another edition and yet another chance to donate a
measly 20p to the greatest club in England. This issue is devoted to Rich
Bradley for slamming in 2 goals last week (you'd better buy the fanzine for that!)
So it didn't seem like Besty's words in the last issue were correct. He was
heard to say 'sorry you'll be making an early cup exit.' To which we replied
'BOLLOCKS!' which funnily enough was the right reply. Don't be at all suprised
to see us gazing into crystal balls and donning gypo scarves soon to predict
the future...
As you may have noticed (unless you are Eddie Avison, Andy Hill, Will Balderson
or Julian Bevan) this issue has all been typed and photocopied, therefore we
are not making any profit at all on this issue. This is because of circumstances
beyond our control, ie. unavailability of a printer (Darren you b****rd)
Hopefully this unfortunate escapade will have been sorted by the next iss.

SHEP FOLLOWS GAZZA

Rumour has it that star Mars Bar man Shep has followed in Gazza's footsteps. Mark
has brought out a record. On the A side is a take-off of Gazza's song 'Fog on
the tyne.' Shep's version is named 'Scum on Thornton beck' while on the B
side Shep does 2 songs - 'The man of many mars bars' and a duet with Brian Best
called 'Why are we so crap'. The video shows highlights of Sheps great career
but it only lasts a couple of seconds. The record is due for release next week
on Beef Stock, Acking and Fatman records.

ANDY HILL IS GOING BALD!

Well its true, after years off slagging off Sneb about his long hair, he's
going bald! Either that or his hairdresser is blind. Andy says, however, that
he's going for the 'Eddie Avison look'. Julian Bevansummed up Snebs new look
by claiming 'I haven't seen it yet but if is anything like Snebber usually does,
it'll be crap!'

MICK BARNES

Barney recently gave us a shock statement saying that Sneb and Fatboy were not
turning up at training. He said he did not know about Shep but that Snebber was
now into Australian Rugby. We can exclusively reveal that Shep was stuffing
himself full of chocolate to top up his glucose level in time for
today's game.!

BALDERSON SLAGGING

Sorry Will but Andy Hill says we don't slag you off enough, you hoofing donkey!
Snebber also wants us to slag off Shaun Dixon but we don't think it'd be wise.

BRIAN BEST

Well what can we say Besty except that Wykeham are shit, they can't play
football, Dale are ace, Richard Bradley is f***ing brilliant, you're in for
the same this week, and we hope you like the front cover!

LIKE FATHER, LIKE SON.

A recent interview with one of Barney's young sons produced this breathtaking
statement: 'What's it like to have a famous Dad?' To which he sensationally
replied, 'I don't have a famous dad!' Get him reading those Shoot mags, Mick!

MATCH REPORTS

DALE v KIRKBYMOORSIDE
AT KIRKBY
SOME CUP OR OTHER
FIRST HALF

Dale had a great first 2 minutes of this game as they did not concede a goal
against their first division opponents. Although Dale were playing well,
Kirkby went ahead on 30 minutes with a crap goal (well it was good actually but
you have to make these reports sound a bit sensational, don't you!)
3 minutes from the half time whistle Snebber was sent through but his nose
got in the way as usual and he was foiled by the 1st division defence. By this
time Dale were doing well to hold their illustrious opponents.
HALF TIME: Kirkby 1 Dale 0
HALF TIME COMMENTS: BARNEY: 'Doing well aren't they, eh?'

SECOND HALF

Thornton again started very well and after 13 minutes Shaun Dixon had a great
chance but the jammy buggers, as Barney described them, kept us out.
Dale weren't to be kept out for long though as with 25 minutes of this half gone,
Will Balderson scored an absolutely brilliant header from an Andy Hill corner.
(What an unlikely combination!) We were in ecstasy but with 15 minutes left the
b*****ds went and scored. This was the turning point of an excellent cup tie and
scuffles were appearing all over the pitch. Also the touch line talk was rather
interesting at this time! (A special Escaped Horse 'F**K OFF!' to all Kirkby
fans). Just as we were coming back they scored again but who cares it was only
a cup match after all.
FINAL SCORE: Kirkby 3 Dale 1

DALE v WYKEHAM
AT THORNTON
SOME OTHER CUP
FIRST HALF

Sorry in advance for this report but due to uncontrolled circumstances Steven
Allerdice had to do this report. (Don't worry, it's edited)
Dale got straight into this one, everyone wanted to beat Besty and with just
10 minutes gone Rich Bradley (No this is not a misprint) drilled the ball right
into the net. Now it says here that 3 minutes later Staurt Hill covered a 30
yard chip very well. A 30 yard chip!!?? Thornton were having all the chances
and just before half time Dale should have been awarded a penalty but Wykeham
were paying the ref too much.
HALF TIME: Dale 1 Wykeham 0

SECOND HALF

Stuart Hill gets loads of praise for a brilliant game it says here (I bet he has
a SHEEPish grin while he is reading this!) A few minutes into the 2nd half
our trusty keeper was booked for supposedly fouling Besty. 23 minutes gone
and the so called Wykeham star player was subbed! Dale were really on top now
and soon brilliant Bradders added a second from a good ball by Shaun Dixon, 2-0
to the Dale. Then they scored I think it says here but it was probably a flukey
goal anyway and who gives a shit if Wykeham scored?
FINAL SCORE: Dale 2-1 Wykeham

Wykeham star player indeed Besty, ho ho!

GEORGE RIPLEY — THE GREATEST REFEREE EVER — A TRIBUTE

Well, we just had to do it sooner or later. Yes, a tribute to the great George Ripley. Many a time we trudged up to the Greyhound Ground expecting a boring game and a defeat against a better side. Precisely our thoughts before the game with Mermaid. But George had this incredible knack of turning a boring game into an explosive encounter. One minute he'd give a penalty when no opponents had been anywhere near the player who dived, then the next time he wouldn't even bat an eyelid when a Mermaid player started to saw off Bradleys legs. Then there were games against Scalby and Scarborians, both of which exploded into controversy because of some dubious decisions on Georgie's part. And who can forget the Ryedale away game where Eddie Avison kicked out at anything but the ball, and Besty was not even booked when he raced the length of the pitch to give Richard Thorner a left hook!

Unfortunately although we scour the fixtures in the Evening News every Wednesday and look down the list of referee's, George has not yet been seen this year. Has he gone into retirement, or is he plying his trade somewhere else? We want George back, you are always guaranteed a good game when he is holding the whistle...

****

AROUND THE LEAGUES

Well as you can see from the league table, we are looking odds on for yet another 3rd place behind RBL and Barrowcliff. Good old Ryedale SC are doing a good job at the bottom and in div 2 it looks like our friends (!) Wykeham are coming down. Funny how they start to struggle as soon as Besty joins them! Old enemy Ivanhoe are mid table in Div 2 but they won't last and will be back in div 3 before you can say 'Snebber is bald.'

Into the dizzy heights of div 1 now, and Mermaid appear to be struggling. The b****rds have probably had everyone sent off by now anyway so they don't stand a chance of staying up. Thought we'd also include the Beckett League, and Slapper Avison's old club Sinnington are recovering from his spell there and finally getting back to normal!

STOP PRESS NEWS THAT WE HAVE BEEN DRAWN WITH SCALBY IN THE NEXT ROUND OF THE CUP.

****

QUOTE OF THE WEEK

'Sorry you'll be making an early cup exit' (BBest before last week's game)

THANKS TO: Rich Bradley for scoring vs Wykeham, Moorlands photocopier, if it was for that you wouldn't be reading this, Andy Hill's hairdresser.
NO THANKS TO: Mark Shepherd for threatening us and telling us not to write about him, Darren's printer, thanks a bloody lot! British Rail for making us miss the Wykeham game.

Scarborough and District League — Division One

	P	W	D	L	F	A	Pts
Filey Town	8	7	1	0	41	6	15
West Pier	8	7	1	0	27	8	15
Edgehill	7	5	1	1	21	8	11
Kirkbymoor	7	5	0	2	18	12	10
Eastfield Res.	8	3	2	1	18	10	7
Cayton Cor	7	3	1	3	14	17	7
Ayton	8	2	3	3	12	18	7
Pick Town	6	3	0	3	15	14	6
Mermaid	7	2	1	4	12	12	5
Seagra	7	1	2	4	9	19	4
Flamborough	8	2	0	6	15	26	4
Ryedale Sp	7	2	0	5	8	22	4
Hunman Utd.	8	2	0	6	11	30	4
Fishburn Ph.	8	0	0	6	9	37	0

Division Two

	P	W	D	L	F	A	Pts
Edgehill Res	8	7	1	0	19	5	15
Rillington	8	6	0	3	28	16	12
Wands	5	5	1	0	20	7	11
Whitby Arcs	8	3	1	4	28	14	7
Fylingdales	8	3	1	4	27	15	7
FC Ivanhoe	6	3	1	2	18	10	7
N Riding Acs	8	2	3	3	10	12	7
Wreyfield	8	3	1	4	16	24	7
Cayton Cor	8	3	0	5	13	33	6
Wykeham	4	2	0	2	5	9	4
Sherburn	9	1	1	7	6	24	3
West Pier	8	0	2	4	6	23	2

SOCCER TABLES

Persimmon Homes Beckett League

	P	W	D	L	F	A
Rosedale	9	6	0	3	22	18
Cuswold	7	5	1	1	30	10
Aswaby Utd	8	5	1	2	27	16
Sinnington	9	5	1	3	23	14
Terrington	7	5	0	2	34	16
Wanders Utd	7	4	1	2	22	14
Amor & Swin	8	3	3	2	24	18
Gillamoor	9	4	1	4	12	18
Slingsby	7	3	1	3	15	15
Kirkby Res	9	3	1	5	18	21
Huby Utd	7	3	0	4	14	18
Ampleforth	6	2	0	4	10	14
Kirkasen Utd	8	1	0	7	7	29
Bagby & Balk	7	0	0	7	5	33

Division Three

	P	W	D	L	F	A	Pts
RBL Res	7	6	1	0	35	8	13
Barrowcliff	8	6	1	1	32	10	13
Scalby	9	5	1	3	21	23	11
Brompton	5	3	0	2	18	12	6
Filey Town	6	3	0	3	13	13	6
Thorn Dale	5	2	2	1	9	9	6
Team Plaxton	5	2	0	3	9	13	4
N Cliff Rang	7	1	1	5	15	21	3
Hun Utd	6	0	0	6	10	31	0
Ryedale SC	4	0	0	4	1	20	0

Division Four

	P	W	D	L	F	A
White Horse	6	6	0	0	46	7
Ayton Res	7	6	0	1	21	8
Eastfield 'A'	5	3	1	1	18	9
RBL Res	7	3	1	3	15	11
N Riding Acs	7	3	1	3	22	27
Wands Res	7	3	0	4	23	21
Flam Res	7	3	0	4	20	24
Sherburn Res	4	2	0	2	13	17
Ganton	3	1	1	1		
Scalby Res	5	0	0	5	8	31
Tenny Utd	6	0	0	6	13	54

THE ESCAPED HORSE

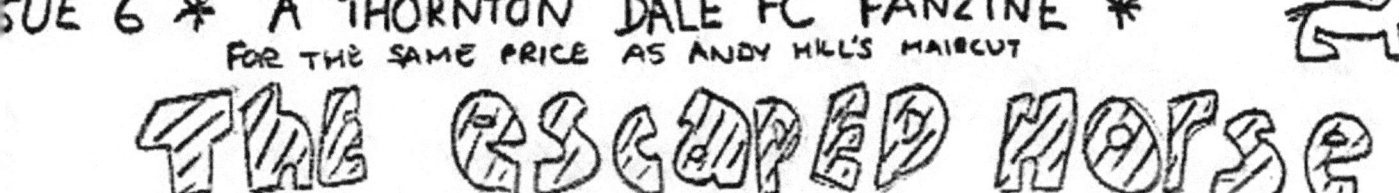

Ooooo! You queer sod!

*Take that you se b***ard!*

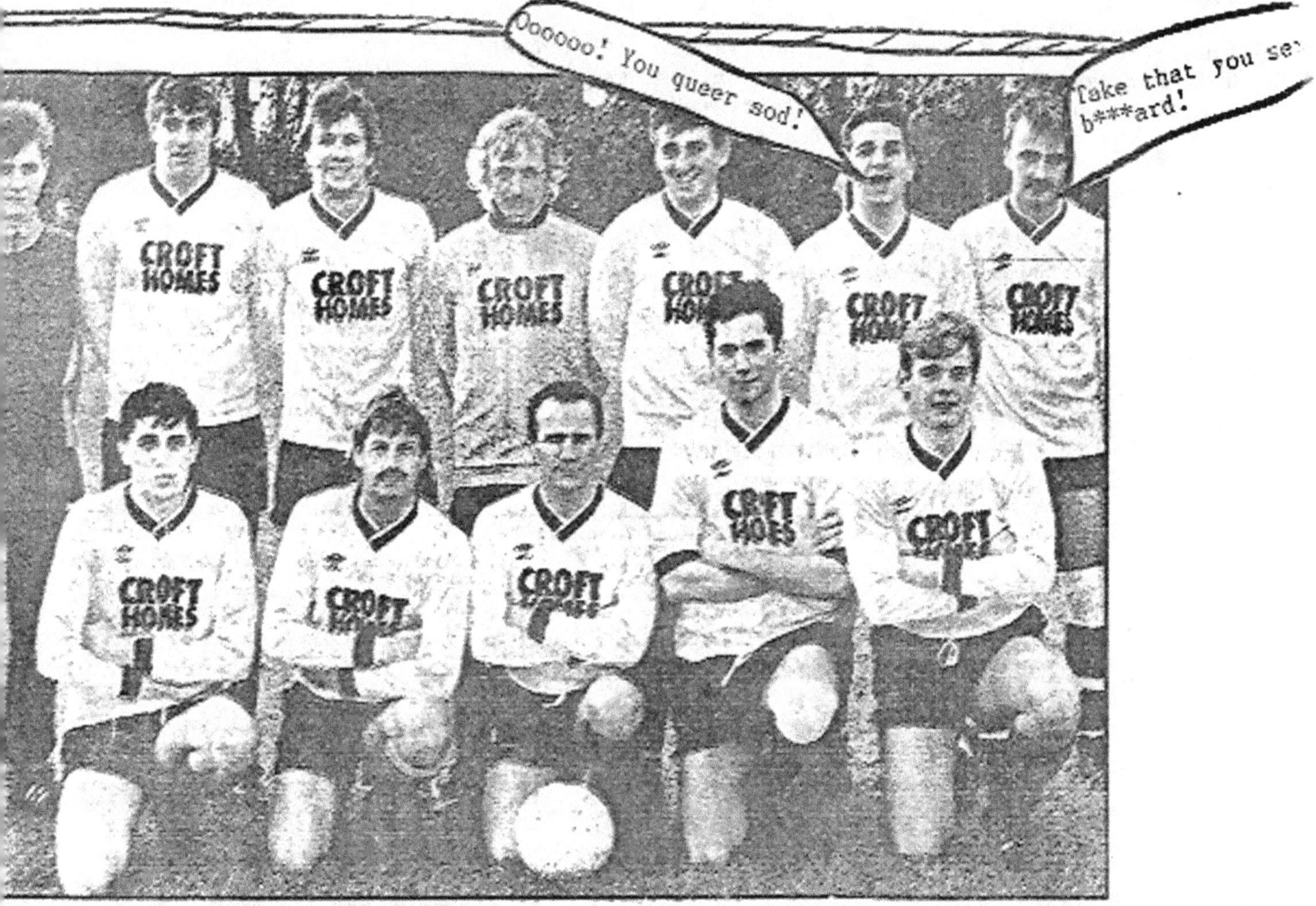

RNTON-LE-DALE: Pictured from back left are

Dean 'I didn't say it honestly Shep' Richardson, Mick 'I'm past this
lark' Barnes, Steve 'F**k off ref' Avison, Stuart 'Where's me sheep'
Hill, Mark 'Give us a mars bar' Shepherd, Andy 'I'm off down under' Hill
Shaun 'Slag me off and I'll smash you shitless' Dixon. FRONT ROW:
Julian 'I'm a jolly good schoolboy' Bevan, R'Sorry don't know you're
full name' Smith, Eddie 'Bald is beautiful' Avison, Will 'Sorry lads
don't have enough money' Balderson, Richard 'Ughhhhhh, F**k off' Bradley

EXCLUSIVE

KINKY TRUTH OF DALE STARS

Greyhound Grapevine

EDITORIAL

Well here goes issue 6 with it's usual variety of Snebber slagging, Best bashing and mars bar eating! After 2 glorious weeks of smashing Wykeham we were back to our usual crap selves last week. We would just like to ask this question: Why are Wykeham in the 2nd division? Also is there any reason why Richard Bradley can't score goals like that every week?
Oh and by the way, just what were you doing to Andy Hill in the photo, Shaun?

****

MARK BAGNELL IS FEARGEL SHARKEY?

Even the Sun will be jealous of this one! Remember that so-called pop star Feargel Sharkey who churned out all those terrible 'hits' a while back? Well he can now be seen in Dale colours under the alibi of Mark Bagnell! Just imagine how much money we'd get if we flogged him back to Stock Aitken and Waterman! We're sitting on an absolute goldmine! Mick Barnes get him sold, we could buy Gazza for that much!
Thanks to Andy Hill's brother for that astonishing piece of observation, oh and by the way don't read everything you read in the papers!

****

KINKY TRUTH OF DALE STARS

Well, you've really been caught at it this time haven't you lads. Well nobody, not even you sly dogs escapes the eye of the Escaped Horse! All your sexy secrets have now been exposed. We always wondered about you Andy, and now all our suspicions have now been proved right! Just look at that face expression Andy, don't try and tell us it was only done for a bet, and we HAVE noticed that Shaun Dixon's hand is out of sight. Anyway lads could you please practice your antics somewhere else in future, it's given this family club a very bad name.

****

DALE ON TOUR?

What's this we hear, Thornton going on a tour of Holland? Please could someone inform us on whats going on, as Mark Shepherd and Andy 'oo-er' Hill mumbled something to us a couple of weeks back about the Dale touring foreign parts.
Well if this is true could we just inform the management about the risks of taking certain players. It is funny how rumours of a tour of Holland blow up to coincide with our 2 star players' kinky antics and also a new law which has just arrived in Holland, which is reproduced below courtesy of the 'Sunday Sport.'
So don't let those 2 go wandering about at night, eh Mick?

TEENY DUTCH kids were given the go-ahead for "all the way" sex last night.

A new law allows sex with girls as young as 12. But politicians who voted for the change by 144 votes to five claimed it was not a perverts' charter for child sex.

****

RAYMOND SMITH IS 'OWER 'ILL'

Hot news from star fan Deggy Bond. During the recent RBL match, Deggy claimed that Ray used to play years ago but is crap now because in his famous words, he is now 'ower 'ill'. Of course we don't believe him and he is marvellous (ha ha!)

****

MATCH REPORTS

Double delight for Dale after two cup wins over top class side

THORNTON-LE-DALE beat Second Division Wykeham for the second successive week in cup games.

After last week's game this week produced a close game with the only goal of the game coming from Richard Bradley midway through the second half.

A pass over the Wykeham defence beat their offside trap with Bradley running on and hitting a great 20-yard shot into the roof of the net. Outstanding for Dale was Julian Bevan.

Well we couldn't be bothered to write a match report for the 2nd Wykeham match, we didn't take any notes because we were too busy slagging off Besty! As for the British Legion game it was a load of crap and you don't want to read about it anyway do you? So that's your lot for this week, we've got more important things to write about!

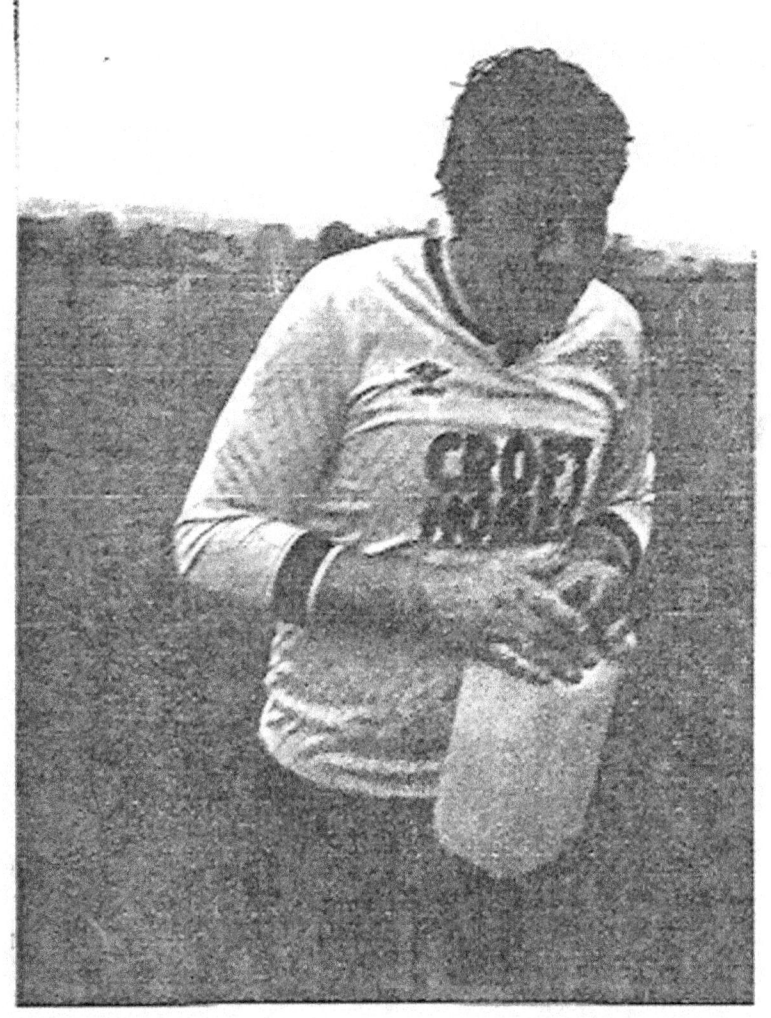

MICK BARNES TRUNDLING OFF AT HALF TIME IN THE 2nd WYKEHAM GAME. QUOTE: 'NO PHOTOS, I'M TOO KNACKERED!'

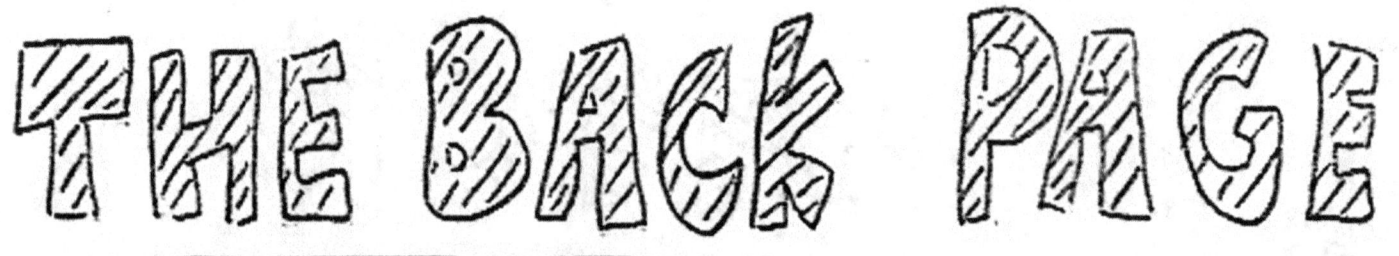

THANKS TO: The bummers on the front for the exclusive pic * Richard 'up yours
Besty' Bradley * Mick Barnes Junior for the comment on Shep (see below) *
Moorlands again for their trusty photocopier...
NO THANKS TO: Mermaid FC, naturally, * The blind referee that sent Shaun Dixon
off * Royal British Legion for coming from the same town as Mermaid * Everyone
last week for playing crap * The management for taking Andy Hill off against
Wykeham * Besty - he actually scored for Wykeham last week but they still lost,
and as we said earlier don't believe everything you read in the papers!

****
QUOTE OF THE WEEK (Well, we're not usually nit-pickers but it's a conversation
actually)

ESCAPED HORSE: Does your Dad make funny noises in the night?
CRAIG BARNES: Yes, he snores!
ESCAPED HORSE: Do you think Shep eats too many mars bars?
CRAIG BARNES: No he eats too many cherries!

(We don't want to sound funny but we don't quite know what the relevance of
cherries is!!

****
BRACKSTONE FOR DALE

Exclusive news from the Dale contingent at Lady Lumleys that Dale will be a player
better off after todays game... We're keeping you in suspense Mike, but you'd
better have remembered the signing -on forms.....

****

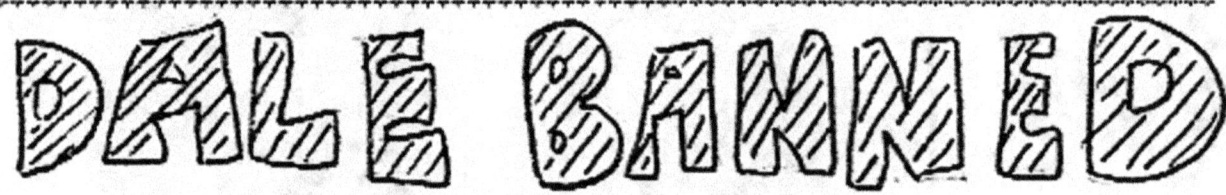

More exclusive news that in a few weeks Dale could find themselves without a
league to play in. News from the Scarborough FA is that referees have complained
about rowdy supporters slagging off the referee and the league have said that
they will give us a few more weeks to sort out this rowdy element of our support
before taking action. We, as noble fans of the club, totally agree with the
FA's stance, but we don't know any rowdy supporters...
The source of this information will remain anonymous so that Steven's dad doesn't
realise that Steve told us!

****

We've suddenly realised that we haven't got much space left and we haven't done
our usual Snebber and Shep slagging. So here goes...
Shep reckons that Andy Hill is moving to London to try and re-unite with that Ozzie
Bird. Nothing to say about Shep this week, except that he's a fat lump of lard
who eats too many mars bars. Ho ho, I bet you thought that we weren't going to
slag you off this time...

FAMOUS DALE SONGS OF OUR TIME:

'There's only one mars bar Shepherd'   Heard at last week's crap Legion game.....

THE ESCAPED HORSE

N GOING DOWN GOING DOWN GOING DOWN GOING DOWN

DALE CRISIS

BEATEN BY ROCK-BOTTOM HUNMANBY * ONLY 6 POINTS ALL SEASON * JUST 9 GOALS SCORED * STAR MAN AVO BOOTED OUT * BESTY BRANDS US 'NON-TRIERS' * BEVAN MISSES GAME AFTER BINGE * DALE LANGUISHING 4TH FROM BOTTOM

O HOPE OF ROMOTION *

SING DOWN?

? ? ? ? ?

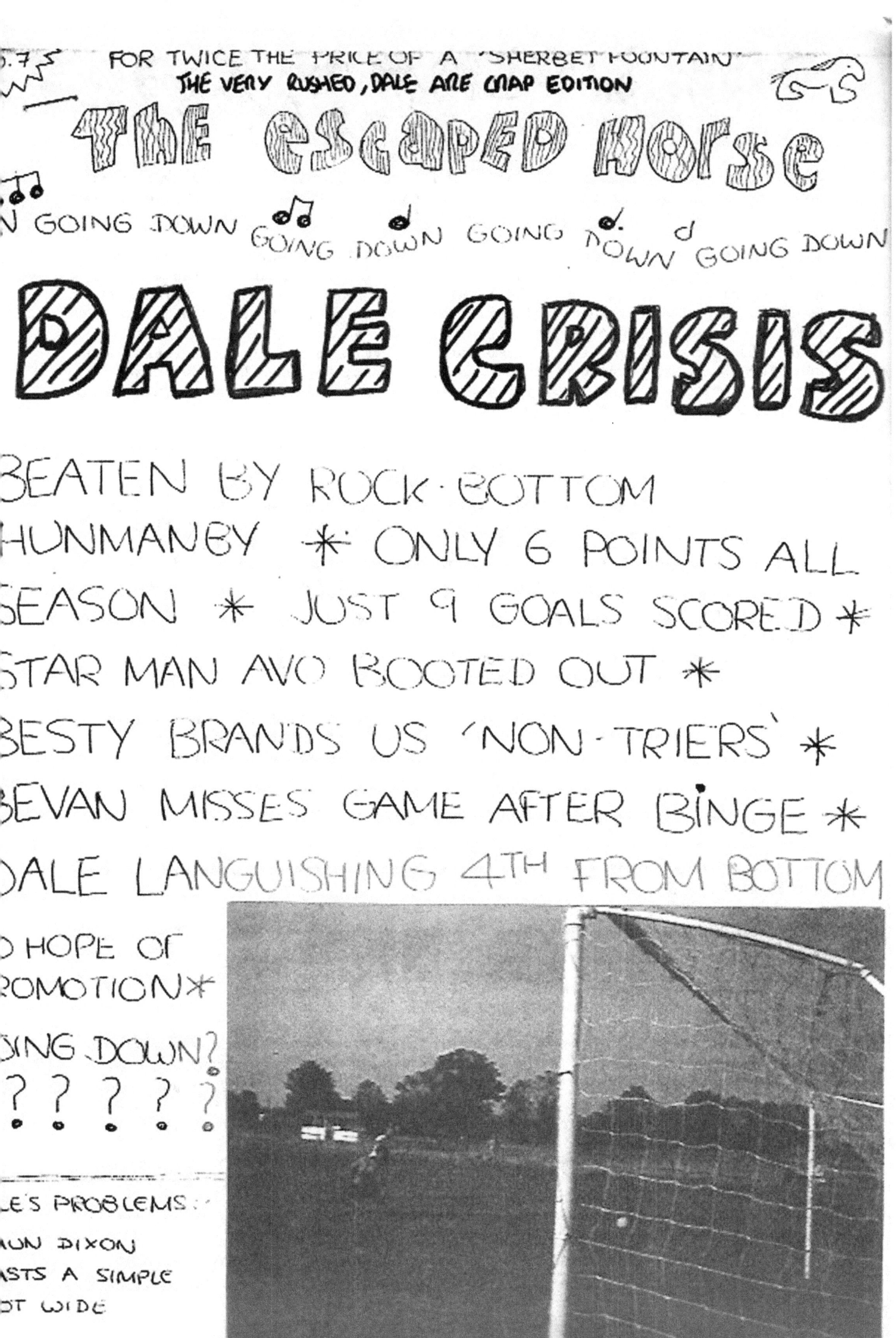

LE'S PROBLEMS:

NON DIXON

ASTS A SIMPLE

OT WIDE

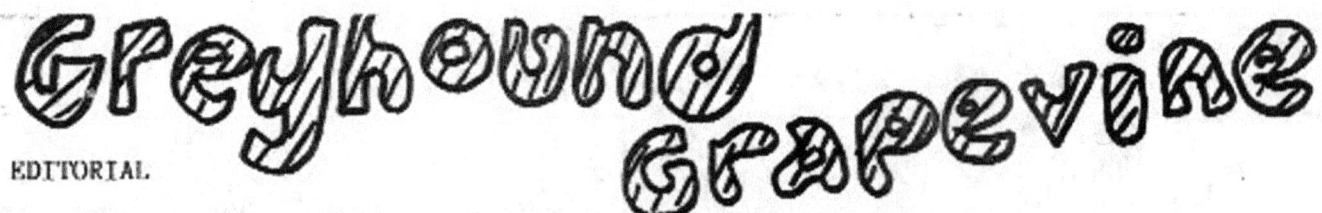

EDITORIAL

To think, we were going to call this fanzine '3rd again.' Perhaps we were wise
not to. This is the first serious piece we have had in the fanzine but we think
it is so important that it should take up the majority of this issue.

This season, discipline and will-to-win has been at it's lowest for many years.
This even prompted star player (we've got to admit it sometime) Brian Best to
quit the club. Although many would argue that we have a brilliant replacement in
Shaun Dixon, we wonder what would have happened if Besty and Shaun had been
playing alongside each other this season? We'd have scored far more goals,
that's for sure. And who is to blame for this? Perhaps not the management, who
can often be heard attempting to motivate the side, although Will Balderson
was complaining to the bosses last week to 'do something.' When a captain says
this sort of thing, something must be wrong.

We do agree with the management's decision to substitute Steve Avison at the
RBL game. However we feel it was wrong to ban him indefinitely from the club.
If he wants to come back at a later date, he should be encouraged to do so.
Getting rid of the more motivated and experienced players and ending up with
a bunch of pansies and lager louts is surely not the way to get promotion.
On the subject of Avo being 'booted out' shouldn't Julian also have been
fined/banned for not turning up to a game because he had a hang-over? This is
more serious than being slightly aggressive on the pitch.

Many will think we are taking things a bit too far now, but what is a football
club formed for? Obviously success is what is wanted, clubs like West Pier and
RBL, who are not much better than ourselves, are achieving successes just
because their attitude is much better.

We are not suggesting that the managers should resign, just that they should
think very seriously before making important decisions, and perhaps try to
motivate the players a little more. 6 points from 7 games with only 9 goals
scored is definitely not the ideal way to start a season.

Perhaps Besty's famous quote of 'Oh, you're crap you lot' is finally coming
true......

****
QUOTES OF THE WEEK

Besty at the recent game when Wykeham lost 10-1 to Cayton: 'oh you're crap, you
lot.'

Andy Thrill: 'Bevan is a big dog's cock!' (just what is meant by this we are not
quite sure, but how do you know Andy? - Eds)

****
THANKS TO: CAYTON CORINTHIANS for thrashing Wykeham...LEE BRACKSTONE for taking
training seriously... DEAN RICHARDSON for turning up to every match and never
getting a game...(talk about loyal)...Psycho Ray Cook last week - very entertaining
...STEVE AVISON...Thanks for the memories.....................................

NO THANKS TO: Whitby Arcadians for losing to Mermaid...the weather at Hunmanby
Mermaid FC, yet again...The FA for trying to ban us (you won't get us away that
easily - see issue 6) Kenny Hill - hope you're not like Andy..............
****

Just to prove that only 'big dog's cocks (quote Andy Hill) do have sattelite dishes,
Andy Thrill and Julian Bevan have both been spotted with these monstrosities on
their tiles...

BEVAN: BOOZE, BIRDS AND BRAINS   A PROFILE

The day that 'Ye Olde Corner Shoppe' was sold was an historic day in the history
of Thornton Dale. True, to begin with all it meant was that some 'Southern
Jessies' had moved in. But as time wore on young Julian quickly became well
known.
Every morning he can be seen at the bus stop, spick and span, not a hair out
of place, eagerly clutching his chemistry folder and desperate to get to
school and continue his numerous A-Level courses.
He can also be seen around the school chatting happily to teachers who no
one else would dare approach, talking about subjects such as 'the effects of
Hitler on modern day history' or 'The merits of Winston Churchill.'
But what a difference a few hours makes. Lovely little (?) schoolboy in the
daylight, but when the moon comes out, as it says in the Frosties adverts,
it brings out the tiger in him. Exclusive revelations were brought to the
surface last week when it was revealed by anonymous sources that Julian couldn't
come to the game against Heworth because he was flat out after ONE pint the
night before! Other people tried to exaggerate this still further by claiming
it was orange juice or even water, but that is just going too far. We'll
stick to the coke.
Julian also works regularly at the Buck Hotel although when he has finished all
his A-Levels, degrees, universities etc. it is rumoured he wants to be an accountant.
Perhaps because he is good with figures! His love life is as active as Maggie
Thatcher. A few weeks ago he was happily in love with someone half his age and
one hundredth of his size. More rumours suggest he did not like to be seen with
her in public so he just popped her into his pocket when he met his friends.
Now on to his other major fault: Chelsea. Yes that's right, Chelsea. Every
morning he is seen in the shop flicking through dirty newspapers to read the
latest news. Headlines such as 'Chelsea crash again' and 'Chelsea on course
for relagation' always stare back at him. Last year he took that great rejoicing
in the fact that Chelsea won the 'Zenith Data Systems Cup'. 'The what?' we hear
you cry. Precisely. When we remind him about Chelsea's exploits in the League
and FA Cups he just blushes and tries to change the subject. Over the past few
years the Blues have lost brilliantly at Scunthorpe (4-1 wasn't it J?) and
of course Scarborough, ho ho.
So there it is. A profile of the Dale 'star' - schoolboy by day, wolf by night.
But don't laugh too much. Remember, as that silly git Jeremy Beadle always says,
next time, it could be you!

****
MATCH REPORTS: This week is the what a load of crap week-read on...

DALE v HEWORTH
Shite is the only way to describe this and it'll be to exciting to talk about it!!!

DALE v HONMANBY
Well we've decided that you played so crap that we'll embarass you by printing
this one. After having to put up with some shit group (compliments of Andy Thrill,
The Blue Nile-what a load of balls) in the car we finally got to the windsweaped
ground to find it was below freezing,especcially prepared for Andy Johnson, and
we were going to have to put up with the shitest football ? ever.
This isn't a very big report as my hands were frozen making it hard to write but
here we go...   10 minutes into the second half they scoredaa crap goal(well
played our defence) AND THEY had all the play. We only had one shot, everyone
was playing crap Shep the most and our feet were dropping off as it was so
bloody cold. Well there you have it WHAT A LOAD OF CRAP!

* SORRY ABOUT THE SPELLING MISTAKES AND THE DARKER
PAPER - THE TYPEWRITER TAPE BUGGERED, AND THE
WHITE PAPER RAN OUT !!!

THE BACK PAGE

AROUND THE LEAGUES

As you can see, the ever reliable Gazette could have uncovered a real scoop – evidence of point and match fixings here folks! Can one of the Gazette Statisticians please inform us how Ryedale SC Res have got 27 points after playing no games and winning all 5? They are bottom, 25 points ahead of Hunmanby! Scalby Res have also benifitted from this strange occurence after playing none but winning 6, drawing none and losing 1 game, they have mysteriously acquired 32 points! Hopefully Mermaid are on their way out of div 1, the same applies to Wykeham in div 2 – after losing 10-1 last week, this is almost a certainty. Dale are set to be playing Ganton again next season at this rate, and who gives a shit about division 4? (Us next season!)

****

Mermaid Banned ?!?

After the FA apparently threatened to throw us out of the league because of our rowdy fans, we've come up with a brainstorm! If you don't see us at Dale in the next few weeks we'll be at Mermaid slagging their ref off, so that Mermaid het banned instead, ho ho!

****

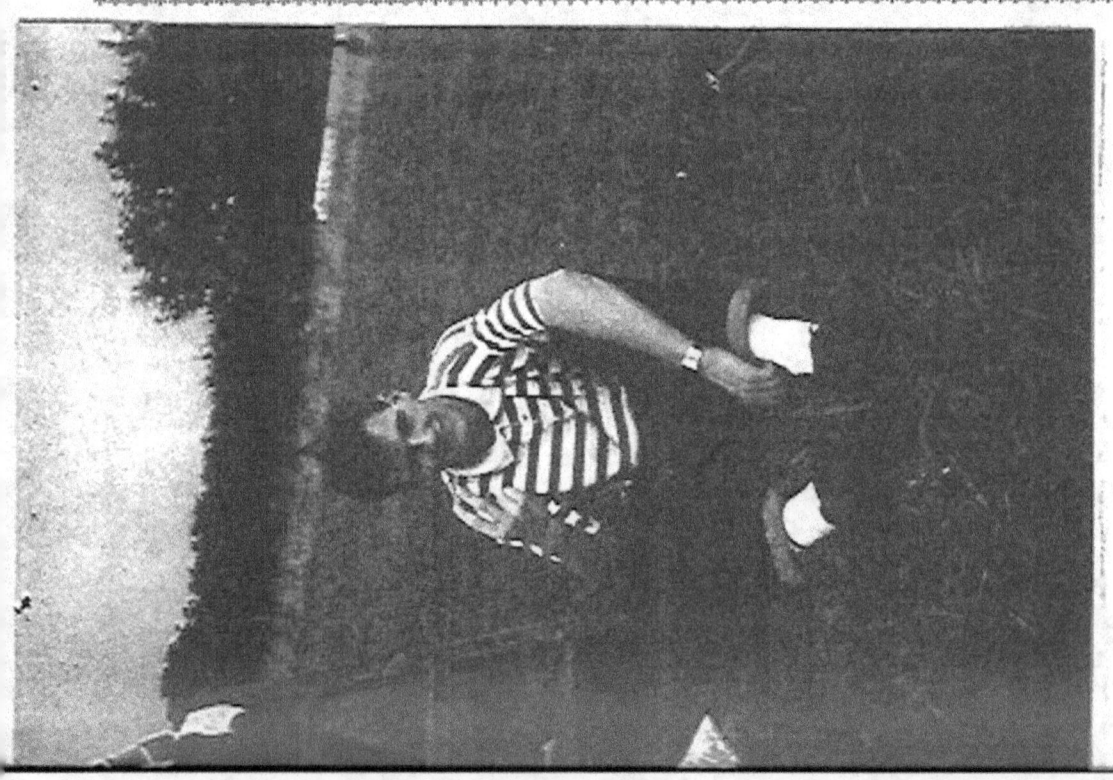

DEAN, SEEN HERE PREDICTING THE NUMBER OF POINTS THORNTON WILL HAVE COME MAY...

ISSUE 8   FOR THE PRICE OF A CRIMBO CARD IN WOOLIES

THE ESCAPED HORSE
CRIMBO SPECIAL

AN UTTERLY MAGNIFICENT THORNTON DALE FC FANZINE GOOD EH?

LET'S ALL STAY OUT LATE AT NIGHT, UNTIL THE PUBS WILL CLOSE, THEN WE'LL SHOVE A FAIRY ON THE END OF SNEBBER'S NOSE !!!!!!!!!!!!!!!

INSIDE: THE SEASON SO FAR THRU THE EYES OF THE HORSE GUIDE TO THE DALE SQUAD * YOUR CRIMBO STARS WITH RUSSELL GREYHOUND * PHOTO'S * MATCH REPORTS * MORE MERMAID MAULING, WYKEHAM WHACKING AND BESTY BASHING * WHAT ELSE DO YOU EXPECT FOR 40p, GREEDY BUGG

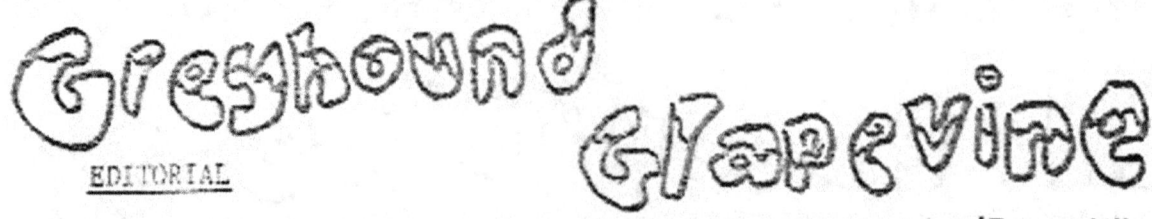

EDITORIAL

So here we are, Crimbo at last. This of course means the 'Escaped Horse' christmas edition, the price is double but this means you get a double edition. We'll be back to normal next time so you scrouges don't need to worry to much. As Dale don't have a game for the next three weeks, including last weeks game, the Escaped Horse have been trapesing around different grounds so expect to see reviews of rival teams in the next few editions. This week we visit our friends and yours Mermaid. All the usual stuff and lots more. Oh by the way sorry about the crap edition last week, we blame Steve Allerdice.

****

BIGGER GOALS?

What's all this, is Colin Moynahan back or something? football goals bigger! If anything surely they should be smaller, why don't the F.A just look at Dales away goals tally? It's bad enough as it is. Then again there is a good side, Andy Hill might score now!

****

MORE GAZZA CRAP

Oh what a surprise, that singer, entertainer, fatboy, football player(?) called Mark Shepherd ooops sorry Paul Gasgoine won the Sports Personality of the year award. Just because he crys in one football match he becomes a national hero (you'll have to try it Shep). What a load of balls!

****

MANAGEMENT UPSET

Shortly after we published the 'Avo never to play for Dale again collumn in the last edition, we here of Mike Aconly complaining to some 'big dogs cock (Julian Bevan) that we should stick to the funny side of things and that he never said anything like that. Well if you didn't notice there is another manager too. As for sticking to the funny side of things well of course we should our side are only rapidly falling down the table, losing to Hunmanby, hardly scoring at all, playing rubbish etc etc. We should be pleased shouldn't we.

****

THANKS TO: The Brompton keeper, Moorlands (we're back there again),Father Christmas.
NO THANKS TO: The left over turkey (sandwiches for weeks), Mermaid F.C, West Pier, Russell Greyhound (we had to pay him loads), Scalby striker Mick Barnes.

****

DONKEY OF THE WEEK/MONTH/YEAR: It wasn't very hard to pick this one, it goes to the famous MICK BARNES (keep banging 'em in for Scalby).

****

QUOTES OF THE MONTH:

Brian Best- "There's no difference between 10-0 or 1-0.
Brian Best- "Our keeper gave up after a couple (so much for commitment.)
Beggy Bond- When asked about the-Dale Mermaid game "I fair clogged 'im one"
Mick Barnes- "I'm knackered"
Mick Barnes fan club- Silence

****

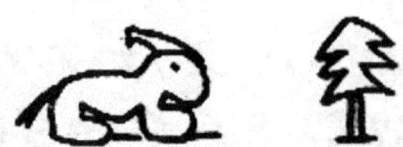
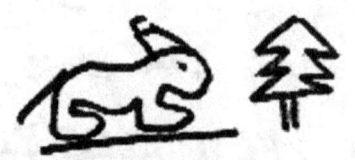

CONFESSIONS OF A BROMPTON 'KEEPER

Exclusive

Hot on the heels of the 'Besty exclusive' comes another interview, this time with the Brompton goalkeeper, Dave Hepplestone. Your roving editorial team really are getting around...

WHAT IS IT LIKE PLAYING FOR A CRAP TEAM LIKE BROMPTON?

'I think you mean what WAS it like. When I first joined Brompton it was a crap team, losing almost every week in the 4th division. Now after hard work, new signings and a new pitch, we are doing well. We're sitting pretty in 4th place in the 3rd division with games in hand on the top 3. Brompton FC has a lot of team spirit and a great sponsor, Manor Garage SAAB. (That's 10 quid for the advert - money conscious eds) These will help us do well.

ARE YOU STAYING AT SNAINTON OR FINDING A NEW GROUND IN BROMPTON? ALSO HAVE YOU GOT A RUDE MESSAGE FOR THE FARMER WHO THREW YOU OUT?

We are very happy with our ptich at Snainton, best thing we ever did. Unfortuneately Brompton don't wish to have a football team (Are you suprised? - eds) or so it seems. I can only wonder how long it will be before our name is changed. As for the farmer, who shall remain nameless, he can take his curved pitch and shove it right up his Massey Ferguson...

WHAT DO YOU MOST ENJOY/DREAD WHEN YOU PLAY THE DALE?

I always enjoy a good hard game. I dread being the better side and still losing as we usually do with you. Dale are a jinx team for us, I also hate being cheated out of 2 points as we were earlier this year. TD are a jinx team for us. (Don't you mean you're crap? - serious eds)

WHAT DO YOU THINK OF OUR GROUND/FANS?

I think you usually get quite a good turn out and it's good to see youngsters interested in supporting their local side. Does Shaun still go? (Who? - bemused eds)

DO YOU KNOW ANDY THRILL?

Yes, I phoned him on 0898 last night (Pervy b******d - disgusted eds)

WHAT ABOUT ANDY HILL THEN?

Yes, I was at school with Andy and had to play football with him, Baldo and Dicko for 5 whole years.

WHAT DO YOU THINK OF THE FANZINE BECAUSE WE THINK IT IS MARVELLOUS?

So do I and don't forget when you write about me, be kind, I'm your best customer.

WHERE WILL BROMPTON FINISH THIS YEAR?

Top of the table, of course (Bollocks!)

WHERE WILL DALE FINISH THIS YEAR?

If they get their act together sharpish (or sheepish in Stuart Hill's case, eds) they should end up around mid table. (Surely not that high - bemused eds)

WE'D JUST LIKE TO ADD OUR OWN LITTLE TRIBUTE: You're a crap goaly playing for a crap team on a crap ground, ho ho.

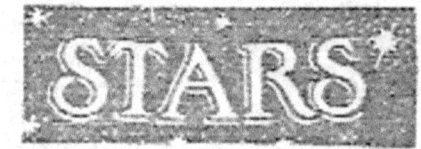 **STARS** by Russell Greyhound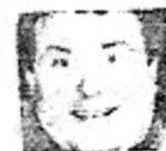

ARIES
(21 March/
29 April)

You will receive a lovely pressie for Chrsitmas possibly from another Dale
player. But be wary, these advances could lead to an exclusive in the next
edition of 'The Escaped Horse'.

CANCER
(22 June/
23 July)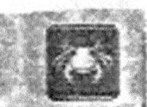

One of Stuart Hill's sheep could go astray and end up creating a memorable
christmas for you. Look out for strange goings-on between Richard Bradley and
your Crimbo tree.

LIBRA
(24 September/
23 October)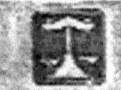

Mesmeric Mercury dwindles it's way into your system and trouble is in the air.
A close encounter with the cross-bar could put your new year celebrations on
ice.

CAPRICORN
(22 December/
20 January)

Watch out! Eddie Avison's head may be mistaken for the christmas turkey, leaving
strange consequences. Arm yourself with sunglasses.

TAURUS
(21 April/
21 May)

A drunk Julian Bevan may create problems for you over the festive season. If
you are armed with a glass of water you will soon put him into a semi-conscious
haze.

LEO
(24 July/
23 August)

They say that too many cooks spoil the broth. Well, too many chocs may spoil your
Xmas dinner, so give 'em all to Shep!

SCORPIO
(24 October/
22 November)

A conversation with Brian Best could persuade you to sign for Wykeham and put
your career on a downward spiral. Avoid him at all costs.

AQUARIUS
(21 January/
19 February)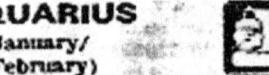

You may suffer a heart attack after seeing Nick Vermont at the Greyhound
Ground. Take some tablets and book a bed at Scarborough hospital.

continued on next page...

YOUR XMAS STARS CONTINUED...

GEMINI
(22 May/
21 June)

Put cotton wool in your ears as a conversation with Deggy Bond may shock you
so much that you end up having triplets.

SAGITTARIUS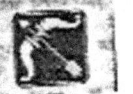
(23 November/
21 December)

A celebration at 'The Buck' may turn sour if you do not see Andy Hill's nose
protuding from behind a glass of Newcy Brown. You could be on a winner on the
fruit machines (Especcially if you are Steve Avison and you kick the shit out
of the thing).

VIRGO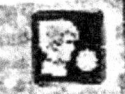
(24 August/
23 September)

A wrong word to Shaun Dixon could prematurely end your career. To ensure survival,
buy him a new football for christmas and kiss his boots every time you meet the
man.

PISCES
(20 February/
20 March)

Watch out for a solid looking Mick Barnes who will flatten you like a steamroller
if you accidently step into his path.

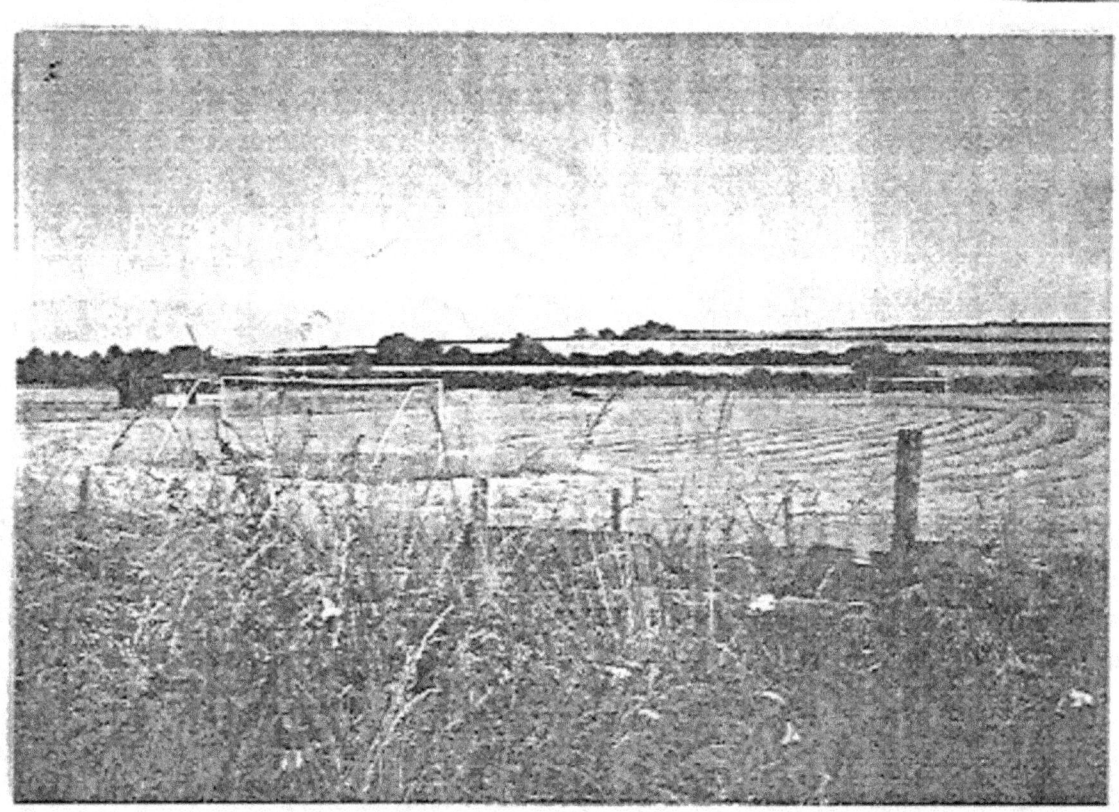

DEFINITELY THE MOST PICTURESQUE GROUND
IN BRITAIN. . . .

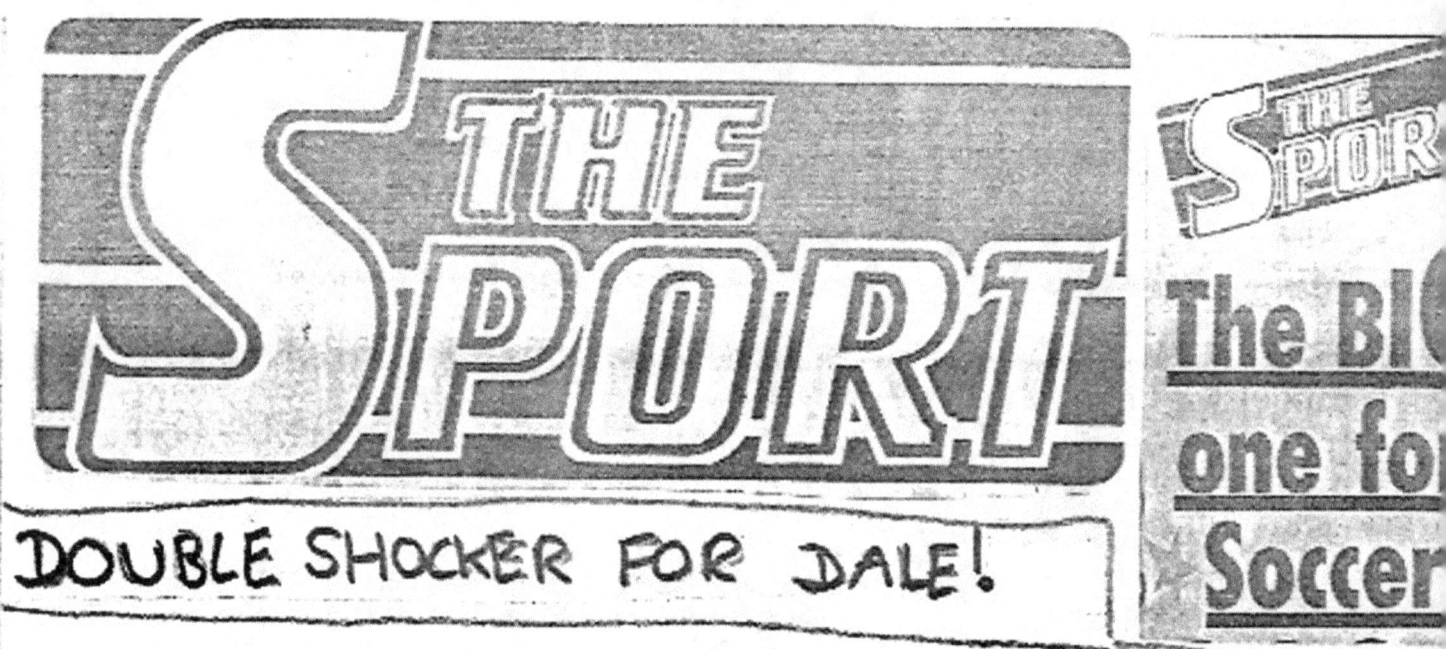

DOUBLE SHOCKER FOR DALE!

MERMAID YOB FOR DALE BOSS

****

ANDY HILL HAS DROPPED A BOMBSHELL
AT THORNTON DALE BY CLAIMING THAT
MERMAID YOB 'CARL' SHOULD TAKE OVER
AS DALE BOSS.

The news comes only days after the
'Dale crisis' revelations in our last
issue. In an exclusive interview
Hill said that Carl should take over
the manager's hotseat as 'we'd be a
better team, that's for sure.'

These revelations bring increasing
strain to the dynamic duo of Barnes
and Aconley to bring in more aggressive
players.

Which is why we have now revealed our
'We want more players like Avo' campaign.
As these players do not come cheaply,
please send us donations, by cheque
or postal order to the address below:
HM Prison Strangeways, Greater Manchester.

Just imagine a 4 man defence made up of
Steve Avison, Rich Thorner, Carl and that
big ruffian Dean Richardson...

MICK BARNES SIGNS FOR SCALBY

****

News just in that Mick Barnes has accepted an off
to join Scalby as their centre forward. Apparentl
the Scarborough side were most impressed with his
goalscoring abilities during the last game betwee
the two clubs.

Although Barney will still be based in Dal, he wi
commu e regularly to the club for training, commu
relarions work etc. in the car which was provided
as part of the signing on fee.

Barney claimed that he was sad to leave Dale but
lucrative offer that Scalby made was too much to
refuse. He said that he needed the money to provi
for his up-and-coming youngsters

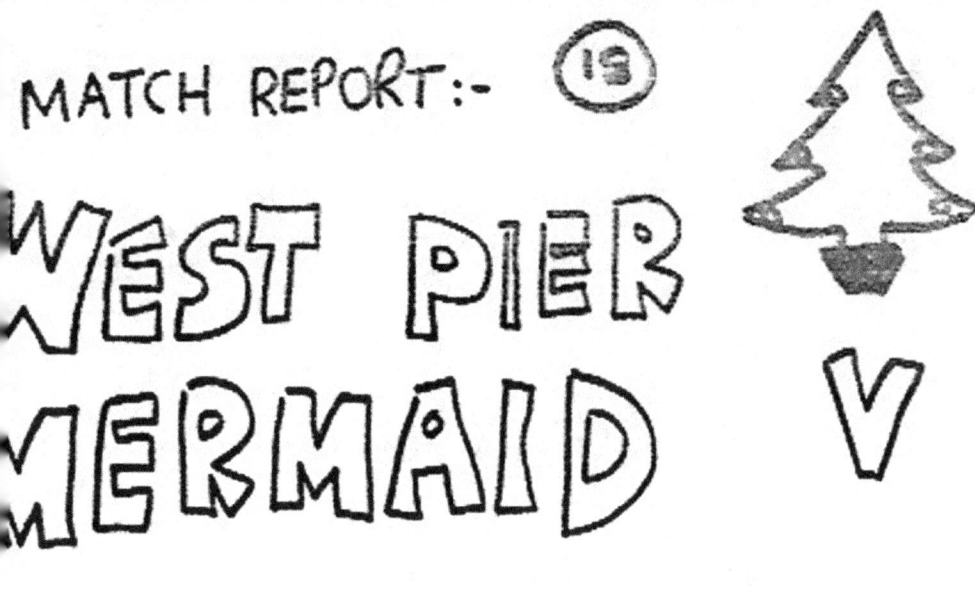

MATCH REPORT:- ⑲

WEST PIER MERMAID V

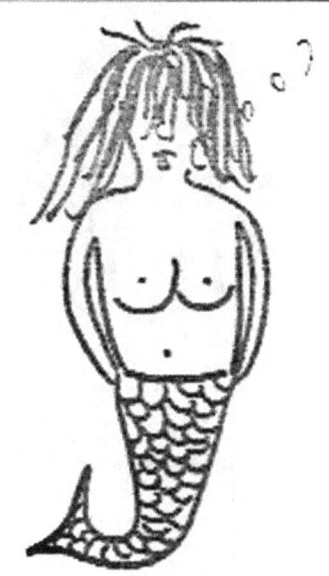

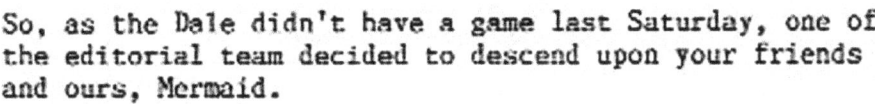

So, as the Dale didn't have a game last Saturday, one of
the editorial team decided to descend upon your friends
and ours, Mermaid.

After all the sheep were finally cleared off the pitch and
the Mermaid convicts turned up a good fight got underway.
After only five minutes Mermaid had given away five free
kicks, what a suprise, the boys from Brid were up to their
usual tricks. The first good chance of the game came for
Pier after someone hit the bar from just inside the Mermaid
half. (Honestly!) The first period was just like you
would have thought it, crap football and plenty of aggro.
Oh what a suprise, ten minutes to half time a Mermaid yob
was booked.

HALF TIME: 0-0

SECOND HALF
The second half started in the same way as the first with
West Pier having all the chances but only good goalkeeping
kept them out. (Sorry, had to say it). Mermaid were playing
their usual standard and soon Pier were straight through
the middle. It was to be a certain goal until that nice
friend of ours, Carl, brought the Scarborough man down.
A certain penalty, but the ref was being paid too much
to let the ref down, so he waved play on. From then on,
West Pier had all the play but couldn't score. Oh what a
suprise, with one minute to go another Mermaid player was
booked!..

FINAL SCORE 0-0

Just goes to show that Mermaid can't play football and ARE
a bunch of yobs...

****
FANZINE REVIEW.

Just a word about a marvellous QPR fanzine recently bought.
Called 'Ooh, I think it's my groin', it is a smallish
zine priced 20p but is well worth the money. They even sent
us 2 issues for the price of 1, and a christmas card.
So get them pennies rattling and those SAE's ready, and write
quickly to: 42a Graham Road, Mitcham, Surrey.

CHRISTMASCHRISTMASCHRISTMASCHRISTMASCHRISTMASCHRISTMAS

Cinema manager Frank Fisher
said: "The committee is paying
for the youngsters' seats and we
are providing the food and other
entertainments.
 "The afternoon should help a
lot of parents who want to get on
with their Christmas shopping."
 The show begins at 2pm.
 The New Year at the Castle will
begin with The Mermaid, show-
ing from January 3.

KIDDIES WATCHING
MERMAID? THE
CASTLE CERTAINLY
KNOW HOW TO LIVE
DANGEROUSLY...

Scarborough and District League

Division One	P	W	D	L	F	A	Pts
...st Pier	12	10	2	0	45	10	22
...ey Town	10	9	1	0	50	9	19
...dgehill	9	7	1	1	27	8	15
Flamborough	13	6	0	7	28	42	12
Eastfield Res.	10	6	2	2	29	12	11
Cayton Corin.	9	5	1	3	19	18	11
Kirkbymoorside	8	5	0	3	18	17	10
Pickering Res.	9	4	0	5	22	16	8
Ayton	11	2	4	5	15	26	8
Hunmanby Utd.	11	3	0	7	17	41	6
Sleights	11	2	2	7	14	31	6
Ryedale SC.	9	3	0	6	11	31	6
Mermaid	11	2	0	7	16	20	6
Fantom Pk Res.	11	0	0	11	12	46	0

Division Two							
Wards	8	7	1	0	28	10	13
Rillington	10	6	0	4	26	21	12
Edgehill Res.	9	6	2	1	21	9	12
Whitby Arcs.	10	5	2	3	35	16	12
Wrenfield	10	5	1	4	20	25	11
Fylingdales	8	4	1	3	32	15	9
F C Ivanhoe	7	4	1	2	19	10	9
North Riding Acs	8	2	3	4	11	17	7
Wykeham	8	2	1	5	8	16	5
West Pier Res.	8	1	2	6	8	27	4
Sherburn	11	1	2	8	7	26	4
Cayton Cor Res.	9	3	0	6	14	36	2

Division Three							
Barrowcliffe	11	9	1	1	49	17	19
Royal Brit Legion	8	7	1	0	38	8	15
Scalby	9	5	1	3	21	23	11
Team Plaxton	7	4	0	3	25	18	8
Brompton	7	3	0	4	15	20	6
Filey Town Res.	7	3	0	4	14	16	6
Thornton Dale	7	2	2	3	9	13	6
N Cliff Rangers	8	2	1	5	17	22	5
Hunmanby Res.	9	2	0	7	16	41	4
Ryedale SC Res.	7	0	0	7	9	36	0

Division Four							
White Horse	9	8	0	1	56	12	16
Ayton Res.	9	7	0	2	38	12	14
Eastfield 'A'	7	5	1	1	28	11	11
Wards Res.	9	4	1	4	31	23	9
Brit Legion Res.	8	3	1	4	17	17	7
NR Ace Res.	9	3	1	5	24	33	7
Ganton	9	2	1	3	11	10	5
Sherburn Res.	9	2	0	3	14	21	4
Flambcro Res.	7	3	0	4	20	24	4
Scalby Res.	7	1	1	5	10	32	3
Tennyson Utd.	7	0	0	7	14	58	0

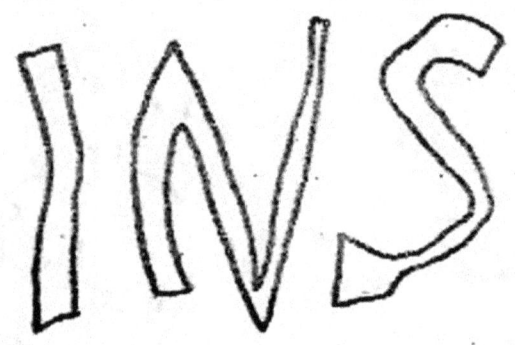 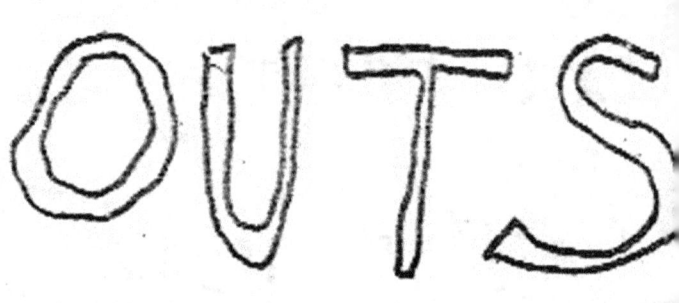

INS	OUTS
New changing rooms	Haircuts like Andy Thrills
Seating accomodation at the Dale	Mick Barnes (obvious reasons)
Sun	Mermaid F.C
Shep records at number one .	Ganton Rangers football pitch
Free photocopiers for supporters	Pig Farms
Five goals against Wykeham	Relagation (ha ha)
Promotion (ha ha)	Two left feet (Julian Bevan)
Donations to The Escaped Horse	Playing away at Hunmanby
Getting Brian Best back	Leeds Utd F.C
Throwing out Brian Best	The great British weather
A miracle	Gazza records at number one
More than a hundred at Scarbro games	Tories
(again a miracle)	Iraq
Coming home from Hunmanby	Turning up late for games (guess who?)
The Raving Loony Green Monster Party	Rowdy Supporters (disgraceful!)
Cameroon winning the World cup in 1994	Nick Vermont (who we here you cry)

****

Player of the Year 1990/

I. s about time to review the current 'Player of the Year' stakes to see who is the leading contender for our coveted trophy come next May...

WILL BALDERSON: Obvious leader at the moment, due to aggressive play all around the pitch (and in the pub!) Watch out Mermaid... .

JULIAN BEVAN: Gets a lot of coverage from the fanzine. Started off terribly, bt is getting better and is now up to the standard of Dean Richardson on a bad day...

MICK BARNES: The 'Gazette' claimed he gave a solid look to our defence, but he is also now a proven goalscorer and the leading contender for the 'goal of the season' award.

MARK SHEPHERD: Now playing up front. Has much potential if he cuts down on all those fatty foods. (In other words, he's crap!)

ANDY THRILL: Player of the Year? BOLLOCKS!

STAURT HILL: After winning the award 2 seasons ago, it's gone to his head, and he doesn't seem to try as hard these days...

SHAUN DIXON: If he concentrated as much on goalscoring as he does on Andy Hill's rear, he'd score hat-ricks galore! Another good bet for the title.

NICK VERMONT: Much as we'd like to present this award to an outsider, unfortuncately only people who frequent the Dale ground are eligible for this award...

****

More next time as we couldn't fit you all on this time.......................

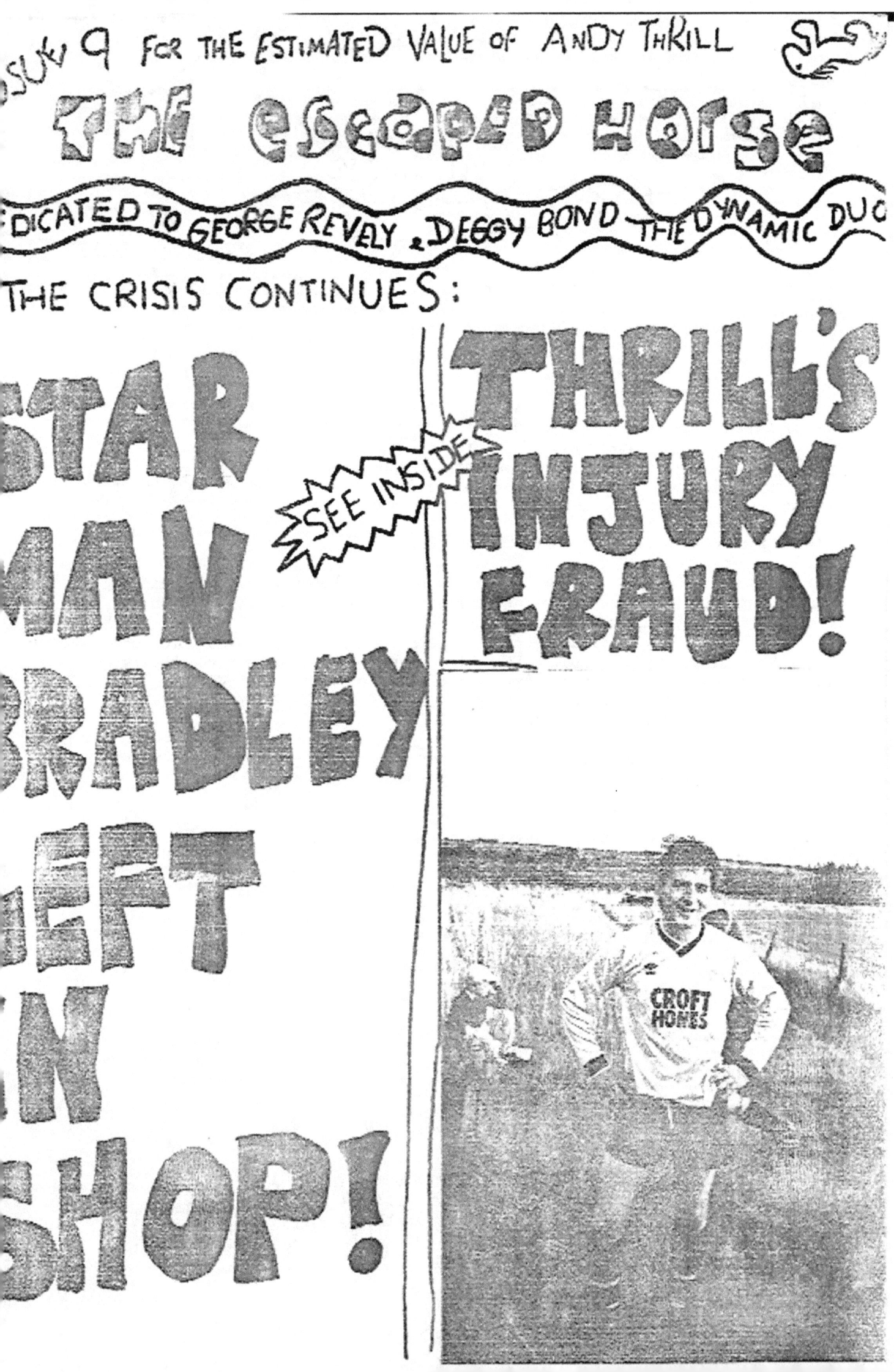

ISSUE 9 FOR THE ESTIMATED VALUE OF ANDY THRILL

THE ESCAPED HORSE

DEDICATED TO GEORGE REVELY & DEGGY BOND - THE DYNAMIC DUO

THE CRISIS CONTINUES:

STAR MAN BRADLEY LEFT IN SHOP!

SEE INSIDE

THRILL'S INJURY FRAUD!

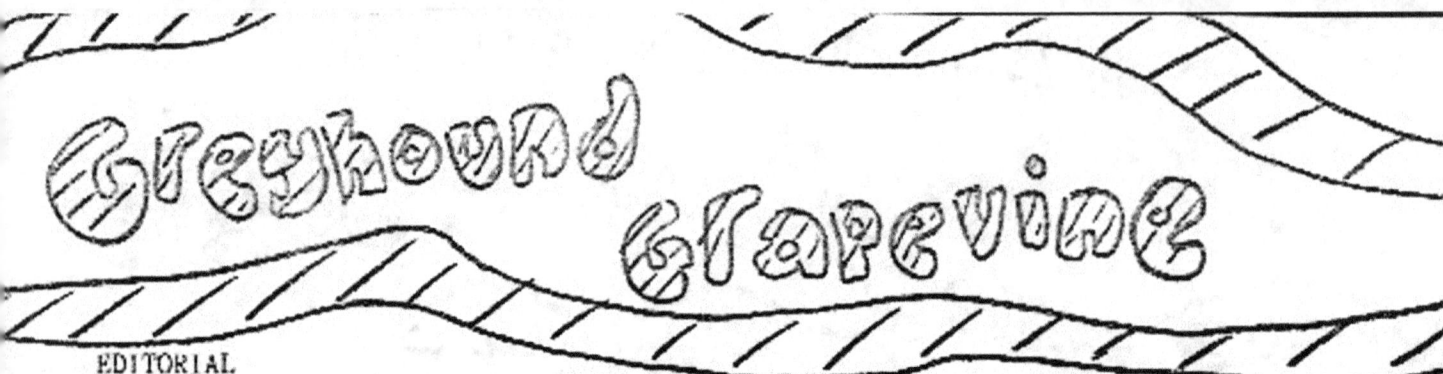

EDITORIAL

So if you're all sober enough after the new year rave ups, here we go with issue 9. It's hard to follow-on from the excellent christmas edition (if you want to buy one we've got some left) but this issue is the same size and 15p cheaper, which really means we scavved loads of money off you last time! However all profit goes to TDFC at the end of season piss up.

ANDY HILL ISN'T INJURED!

Shock revelations that Andy Hill isn't realy injured as the management seem to think. This exclusive news was found out in a conversation with the great man (?) outside the same shop where Rich Bradley had been left standing a week earlier. Thrill claimed that he was taking time off to play golf and that he 'wasn't going to Hunmanby, because it's too windy'. We smell a case of deception here, what are you going to do about it Mike?

BRADLEY LEFT STRANDED WITH CAN OF COKE AND READY SALTED CRISPS

Well Bradders has been a naughty boy then hasn't he? Popping off for something to munch on the eve of the important game at Hunmanby, he paid a hefty price returning outside to find an empty street! But what's more shocking is that they only realised when they got to Hunmanby that he was missing. We know Bradders isn't the most talkative person, with a few grunts stretching his vocabulary to extremes, but surely the thick c**ts in the cars would have noticed an empty seat! After all this commotion he played crap anyway, so lets leave him outside every week till the end of the season!

WORLD SHOCKER! BESTY SCORES

Wykeham gave their best display of the season in beating Wreyfield 7-3 away with goals scored by Brian Best (2), John Agar (2), Michael Robinson and Jeff Goodwin.

← SURELY THIS WAS A MISPRINT?

There was a good second division game at Wykeham with visitors Fylingdales happy with a point from a thrilling 2-2 draw. Brian West put Wykeham ahead after 15 minutes, Fylingdales equalised after 30 minutes, just before half time Ian Lambert scored a rare goal to restore Wykeham's lead. Midway through the second half Fylingdales equalised.

← THIS CERTAINLY WAS!

Big Dale job goes out

Does the trusty Gazette know something we don't know? Is Mike Aconley the new manager of Hull? Has Mick Barnes really left to join Scalby? Have Andy Thrills comments in issue 8 that the Mermaid yob 'Carl' is to boss Dale been proved correct? Remember, you read it here first!

* * * * * * * * * * * * * *

DEAN SPEAKS OUT:
SHAUN DIXON IS A PSYCHO

WORLD EXCLUSIVE

At last someone had the guts to speak out about our very own Vinny Jones, Shaun Dixon. The young Dale schoolboy Dean Richardson spoke his mind about our Brian Best replacement claiming that 'SHAUN DIXON IS A PSYCHO'. The Dale youngster revealed his sensational thoughts after a so called 'training session' in Pickering Sports Hall. Dean claimed that Dicko was running wild, kicking everything in sight, and that he wasn't afraid to view his thoughts with the press because what he said was perfectly true and everyone knew it! But this is certainly not the most shocking aspect of the story, as Dean, who is said to be deeply distressed at Mr Dixon's foolish behaviour is taking it one step further and is going to battle it out in court! Richardson has decided to use loyal friend an' school chum Julian Bevan as his lawyer. Bevan is well known by many to lead this amazing double life, we found out only recently after the cutting below appeared on the front cover of the Northern Echo...

> Rodney Whitchelo allegedly injected caustic soda into Heinz baby products — five times the amount needed to kill — and put parts of a razor blade in a baby food jar.
>   The blade fragments got into a child's mouth, said Julian Bevan, prosecuting.

(SORRY DEAN, WE JUST HAD TO PRINT IT, HOPE YOU DON'T GET DONE IN TOO MUCH, HEE HEE)

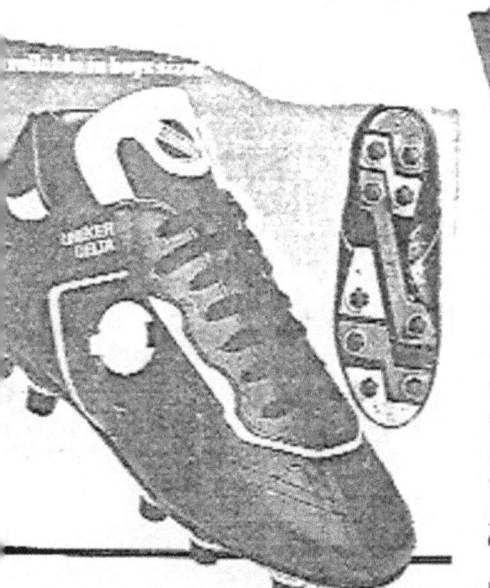

VIC'S BACK!

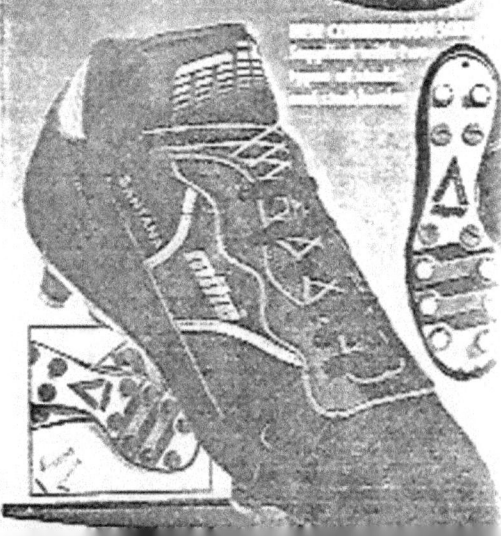

Yes it's true, amazing news that star man Victor Welburn could be back! Vic recently said that 'if I ger' a new pair of boots I might play again'. So just to encourage our star player to get back into the game we have set up our own little catalogue. And we would like some donations for Vic's new boots

THE BESTY LETTER

Well, we really are getting around, aren't we? A few issues ago we had the Besty exclusive, and before you can say 'Wykeham are crap' we've got another one! This was all written by the man himself and is reproduced below word for word...

Many thanks secret source for the latest issues of the fanzine, once again they make for compelling reading, it seems to me if anyone can get this sleeping club going in the right direction, it's you eds? Your horse reporters must have read plenty of Beano's to gain their football knowledge as they've been Dale supporters all their lives! Speaking as one who knows the game inside out (bollocks - eds) stick to the touchline lads, the power of the pen will always find you a scapegoat. I'm pleased to have been involved in the Dale's high point of the season (winning a game) by giving them victory in our clash, it was no hardship for us as we are just rebuilding our side ready for an assault on these trophies over the next few years. On the day we sadly missed our class players who were out injured. If they had been involved, our class would have overcome the Dales' rough tactics ie, kick and run (what's wrong with kick and run? look where it got Wimbledon! - eds)

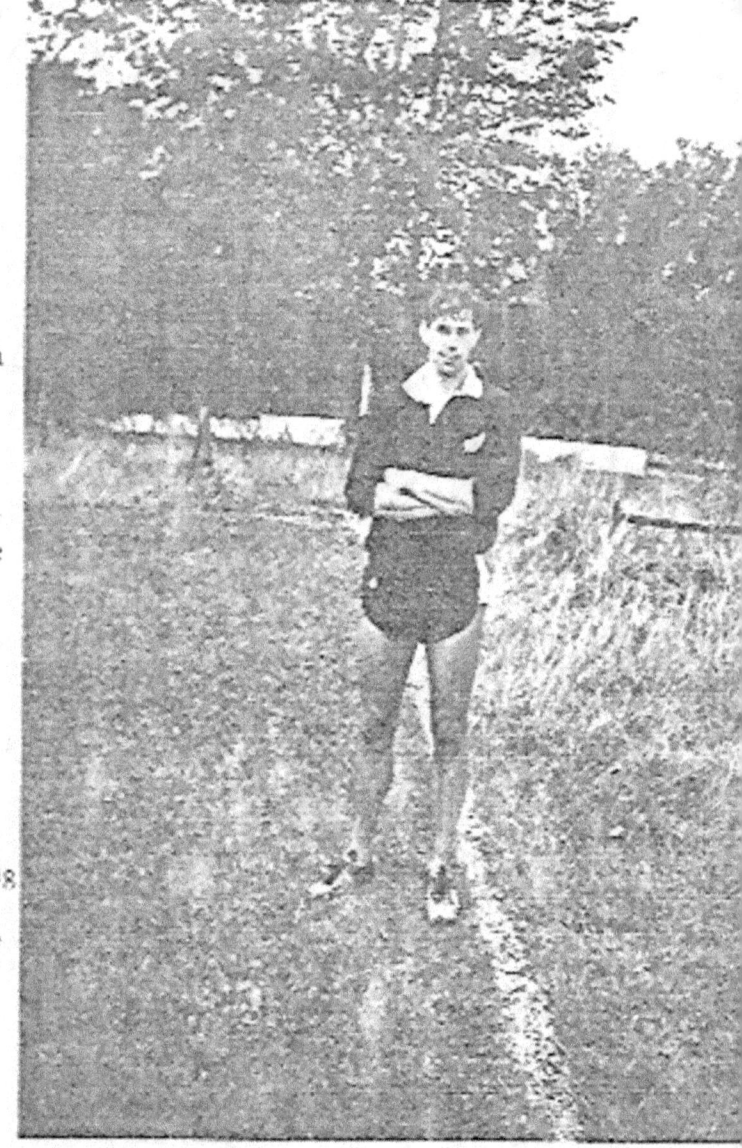

still, it's a pity your forwards failed to turn up for the next round, your club needs to realise it needs to win more than one game to become a success. Can I take this opportunity eds and use your circulation to publicly thank Wykeham for saving me from another desperately disappointing season at the Dale, it's been a real pleasure playing class competitive football again, I'm hoping our christmas programme will bring in the crowds and see us bag some points in our quest for div 1.
Finally wishing you all the best in the new year eds, unlike your team I'm sure the Escaped Horse will never be caught

                    BB

PS - Keep on writing rubbish lads, it goes hand in hand with your team!
PPS - drop me a line if you want to know how to score 7 away and take the points.

I have enclosed some dosh lads for some more never to be missed hard hitting the one that the pro's read Escaped Horse copies. I do realise you're on a tight budget or I wouldn't charge you for my contribution to the mag. However keep the slagging low key lads (never - eds) or my contributions wouldn't come.

                    Cheap,

                    BESTY

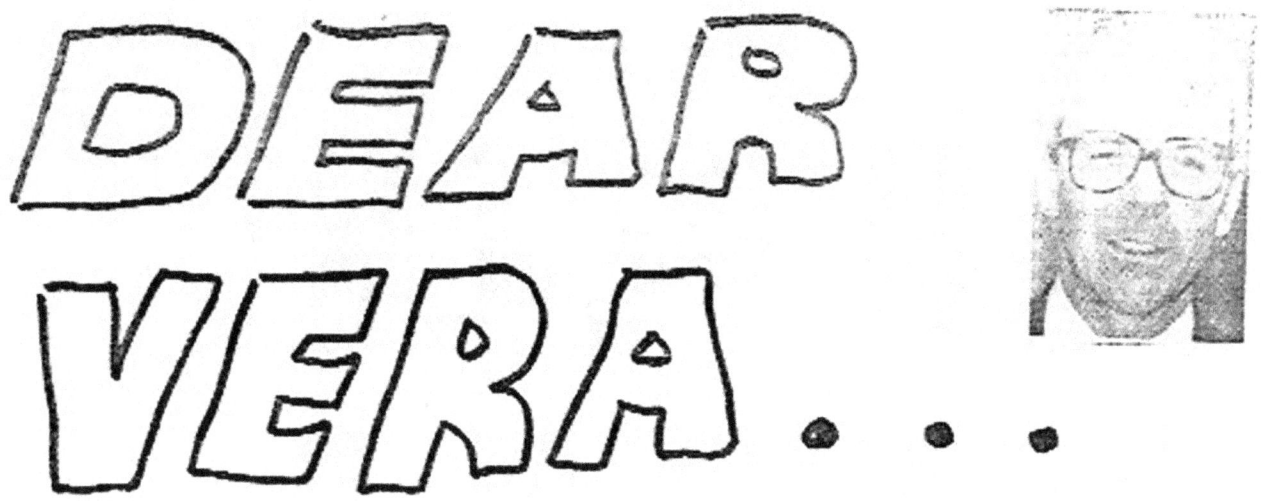

DEAR VERA....

YOUR VERY OWN PROBLEM PAGE

DEAR VERA,

I am in a dreadful situation. You are the very last person in the whole wide universe that I can speak to. The others just push me away. I am deserted, lonely, without a friend in the world. On forty separate occasions now I have dangled helplessly on a rope from the Valley Bridge, attempting to hang myself. To show how much of an outcast I am, on the last six suicide attempts, passers by have tried to help me, even a policeman tried to cut the rope once!
You see, the reason for this is... well, everything. I have spots as big as golf balls (yes I bear a striking resemblance to Andy Hill) my hair is falling out and that which remains is turning green. Half of my left arm is rotting away and I do not have a right leg now after a bungled suicide attempt involving a carving knife. In the last week, I have asked no less than 500 women to give me a date. Each time they have refused. My house was burnt down and 'scummy git' was painted on all the walls. Even my Grandma, ever loving in the past, called me a 'stupid w***er' the other day and threw me on to the street. I used to be married too. That failed before we had even gone out of the church after I tried to advance a little too quickly. My social life is is tatters. I now just sit holding my begging bowl with my one good hand and I watch the youths with their women walking by, flashing fivers at me and spitting on me. Last night I ran out in front of a car to get away from a mob who were chasing me. Instead of slowing to let me cross, it accelerated, throwing me over the bonnet and into a lake where the ducks began to go mad. One passer by yelled, 'Look at that perv in there, he's trying to shag the poor things!' Upon which a man waded in and beat me to a pulp. I crawled back to my spot on the pavement to be met by another beggar who looked down on me and said 'Piss off you lower class scumbag'. I have tried everything. I have tried suicide as I say but I have failed.I don't know what to do. My brother is a millionaire but he won't give me any money. Please, please,please,please,please,please, I need help!
Now you have been filled in on my background, the real reason I was writing to you was to ask you for help on a particular thing, I am a Mermaid supporter.

VERA ANSWERS I was going to give you a good answer until I read the last line. Sorry, your life is doomed. Once a Mermaid fan, always a Mermaid fan. If I were you I'd put myself out of my misery and sit down in front of a steam roller.

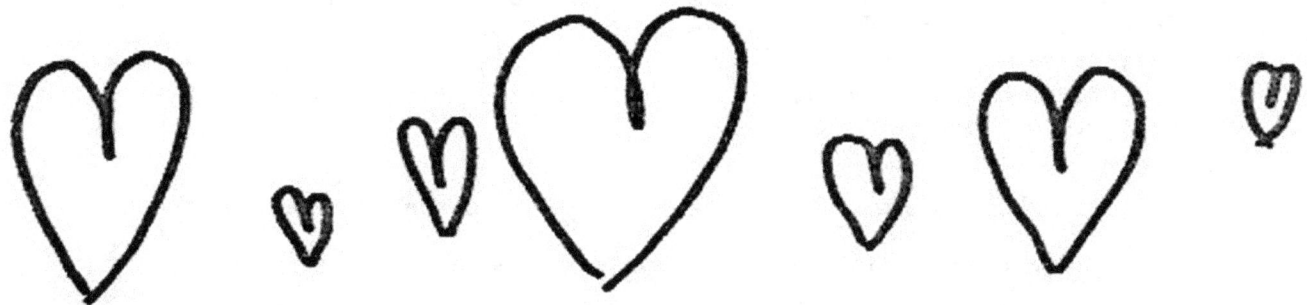

OLD FOLK: SAFETY A CONCERN

With all the frosty weather around at present, slippery roads, sub zero
temperatures, high winds, lashing rain, metres and metres of snow etc;
the media are apparently becoming very concerned for the welfare of our
veteran trio, namely Mick 'solid' Barnes, Eddie 'where's your hair gone' Avison
and Raymond 'ower 'ill' Smith. This recent extract appeared in the 'Citizen'
for whom a spokesman confirmed, 'With all the terrible weather around at present
we are aiming to make people aware of the awful consequences Saturday afternoon
football players have, especcially the old folk who you have mentioned above.'
Take note you three, we think it's better to retire now than battle onwards and
risk like and limb in the treacherous conditions...

****

THORTON FAIRY TALES
by Enid Blyton
JUST FOR LITTLE ANDY THRILL

Once upon a time on a sunny saturday morning Snow White was at home
with the seven dwarfs. The dwarfs wanted to go and see a football match and
eventually Snow White agreed, provided they were back by six o'clock.
  By seven o'clock there was no sign of any of the dwarfs then Snow White heard a
voice in the distance signing "Mermaid Mermaid Mermaid". Ah well, thought Snow
White, at least Dopeys back.

Hope you liked that while you were drinking you're little mugs of coco in front
of the fire!
****

PHOTO CALL

NUMBER ONE:
NICK VERMONT

On your left you see a photo of Dale
star Nick Vermont spotted at the Greyhound
Ground on one of his rare visits here.
As the photo shows...... A slight hitch
here folks, as Mr Vermont seems to have
vanished! Well, we did say it was a RARE
glimpse, didn't we! It must have been
too much to ask of the man. After all if
he had have stayed we'd have got a world
exclusive by now. Oh well.

THE THORNTON DALE FC COACHING GUIDE

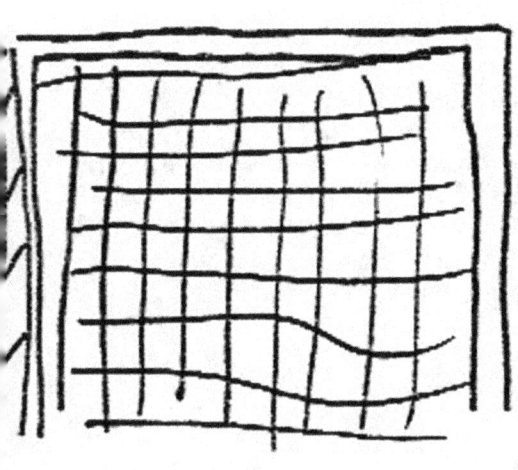

THIS IS A
GOAL. THE
AIM IS TO
KICK THE
BALL INTO
HERE SO
THAT YOU
CAN WIN
THE MATCH.

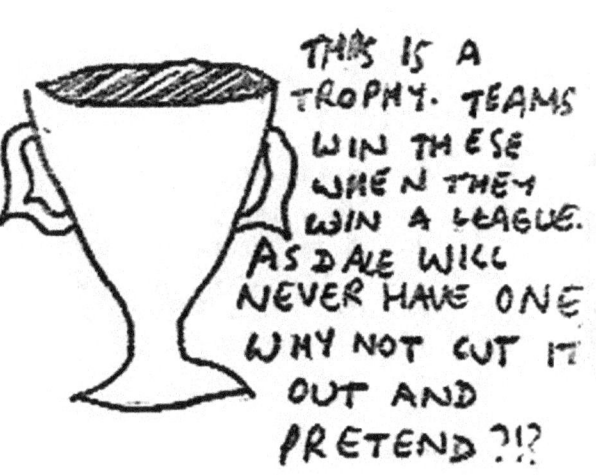

THIS IS A
TROPHY. TEAMS
WIN THESE
WHEN THEY
WIN A LEAGUE.
AS DALE WILL
NEVER HAVE ONE
WHY NOT CUT IT
OUT AND
PRETEND ?!?

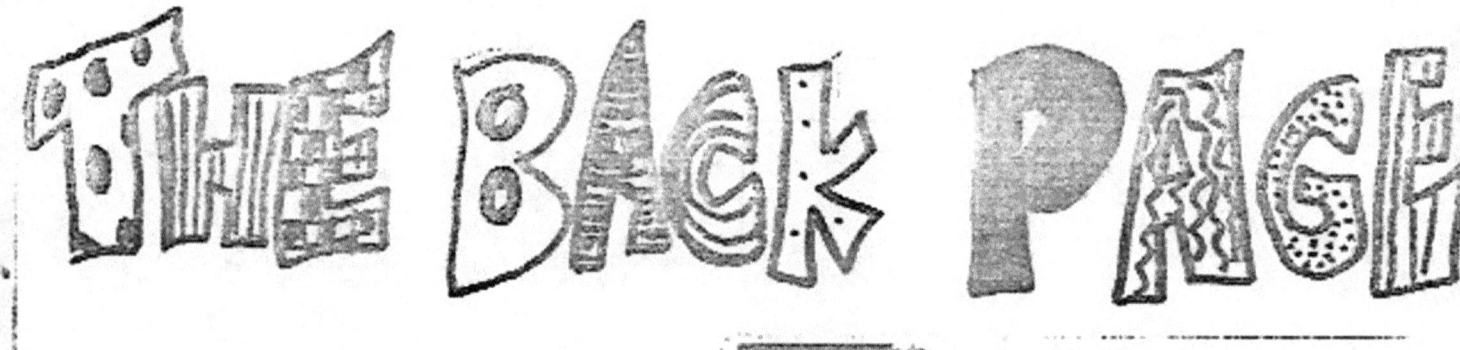

THE BACK PAGE

THE SAVIOUR RETURNS

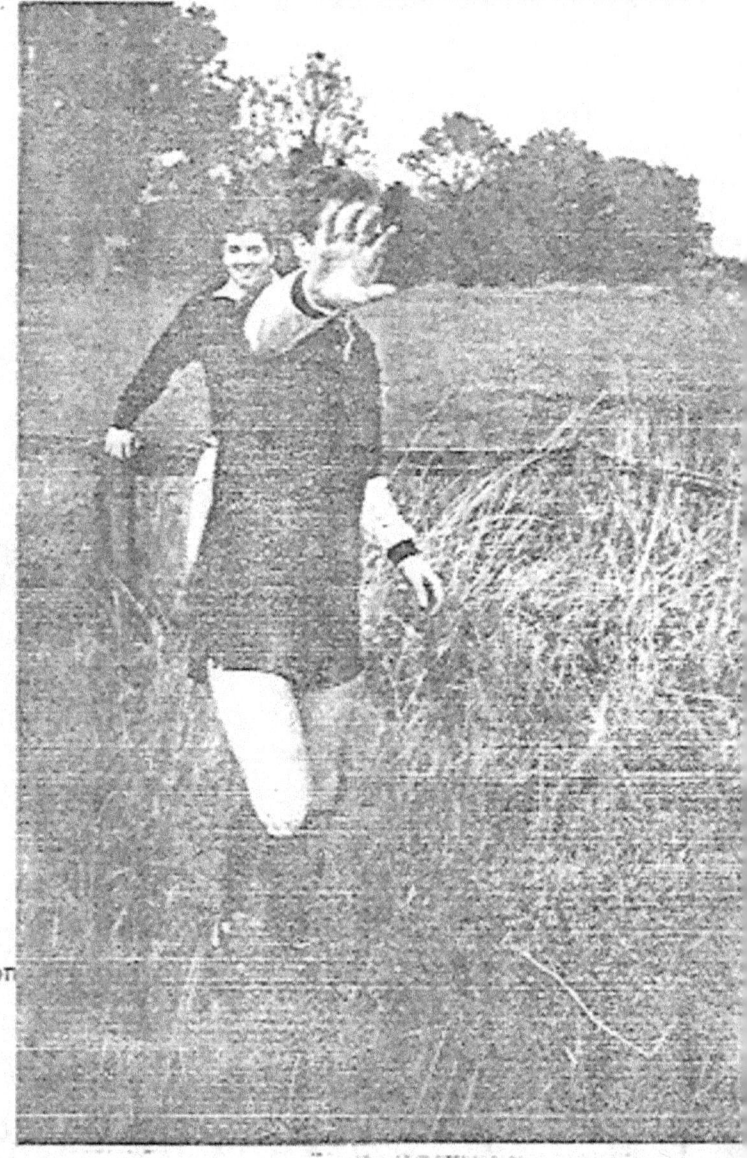

Yes, as you all know by now, except you thicko's like Andy Thrill, our star striker Glen Baskeyfield has finally seen sense and returned to the Dale. With Dicko and Glen forming a strike partnership up front, does this mean the start of great things? Will Glen be our saviour? Will great things start to happen, we could continually get promotion and be in division 1 by 2000/1! Just imagine, Liverpool 0 Thornton Dale 1 - Baskeyfield scores for champs who retain unbeaten record as Liverpool slump to tenth successive defeat. Dreaming? Only time will tell..................

Mick Barnes tells us of strange goings on between Mark 'mars bar' Shepherd and a beer glass in the Buck. Apparently Shep just picked up a glass and lobbed it over his shoulder! However we have an explanation for this. As Shep picked up the glass he saw a little alien face in the bottom. 'Give us a f**king mars bar' mumbled Shep in a drunken haze. When the alien refused, saying he only had low fat yoghurt on the menu, Shep thought he was taking the piss and decided to throw him away! This is only one possible solution, we would like to hear any other stories from people who think they know the real reason. Maybe even from the man himself? We doubt it...

****

That's all for this week then folks, oh and a merry christmas for 1991 in case we forget

THE escaped HORSE!

BANG!

ALSO INSIDE:
ALE IN THE YEAR 2010 IS A POET
SHLEY LOADS ON A
WELBURN LOADS MORE

AIR POLLUTION

CRAP CAVALIER

Dead Hedgehog

EDDIE IN BUS BUS BASH

Greyhound Grapevine

EDITORIAL

Bloody hell, shock horror, we can actually start of a fanzine with some good news!
Now you've recovered from reading that here is the good news: Thornton Dale football
club have won a game! Even though it was agaisnt Ryedale we'd like to thank everyone
who played in that game and just say keep it up (some hope). Anyway read about that
later in this issue. This edition brings the usual brilliant features and also
some great new stuff i.e a lovely poem writen by a member of the famous Welburn
family. Just a note to the managment before we let you get on with the marvels
inside, 'don't leave Bradley in Garbuts this week and good luck.

VIC GETS NEW BOOTS

It's true the famous man himself told us last week. Good old Vic could be back
very soon banging 'em in for the Dale (take note managment). After Victor saw our
dismal attempt in the West Pier game he decided to actually get some new boots!
All we can wonder now is could Vic also do with a new pair of legs, and how much
dirt he'll scuff up on the mount.

BALDERSONS CAFE IS A RIP OFF

A quiet sunday afternoon and two starving young reporters are trapesing round the
deserted village of Thornton Dale in desperate need of food.'Costcutters' says
one starving mouth, Garbuts says another but all is shut. Suddenly the youngsters
remember a small grim hole in a wall pointed out years ago to them by a tramp
Baldersons Cafe. At last food. The reporters trundle in to see a dirty looking
man behind the counter, 'Yeh' he grunts but the lads carn't see anything worth
eating accept two dusty mince pies. They pay and leave. Now back to reality,
what a bloody jew 21p for a grimy mince pie, and not a sausage roll in sight.
Surely you can do better Baldo shape up.

OZZIE'S PART TWO

You may just be wondering why Andy Thrill has had a grin on his face over the
last couple of weeks well we know why. It seems two familiar Australian faces are
back in the Dale. You may think Andy is pleased with this but after the Escaped
Horse revealed Andy's little fling with Shaun Dixon we know this is not true.
The reason for Thrill's smiling face is that he hopes through the ozzie girls he
may meet some hansome Australian men!

THRILL FOR CRICKET WORLD

Staying on the subject of Andy Thrill it seems his injury was a fraud. The reason
why the once Dale star player lead us astray is that he is going to play cricket
for Leeds over fiftys war veterans. This astonishing news was revealed in the famous
Thornton Dale pub, the Buck. Thrill himself told us the great news that he'd be
leaving the club and we wish him all the best in his remaining fragile years at
the slum they call Leeds.

QUOTES OF THE WEEK

Eddie Avison-'Shit, where did that bus come from'
Any Dale supporter- 'Bloody 'ell we've scored'
Mick Barnes- '1991 is the Dales year, the year of the donkeys'
Andy Johnson- 'Sheffield Utd have more points than us'

THANKS TO

Poet Ashley Welburn
Andy Thrill-for the photos
Eddie 'bloody bus' Avison
Andy Thrill again-for leaving
Moorlands-even if it is a rip off

NO THANKS TO

The typewriter tape which nearly ran out
Mermaid F.C-just for a change
Richard Bradley-have you bought a fanzine
yet?
Iraq

Message to Will Balderson-it wasn't really that bad, hope you don't lose to much trade.

But remember it all makes good reading.

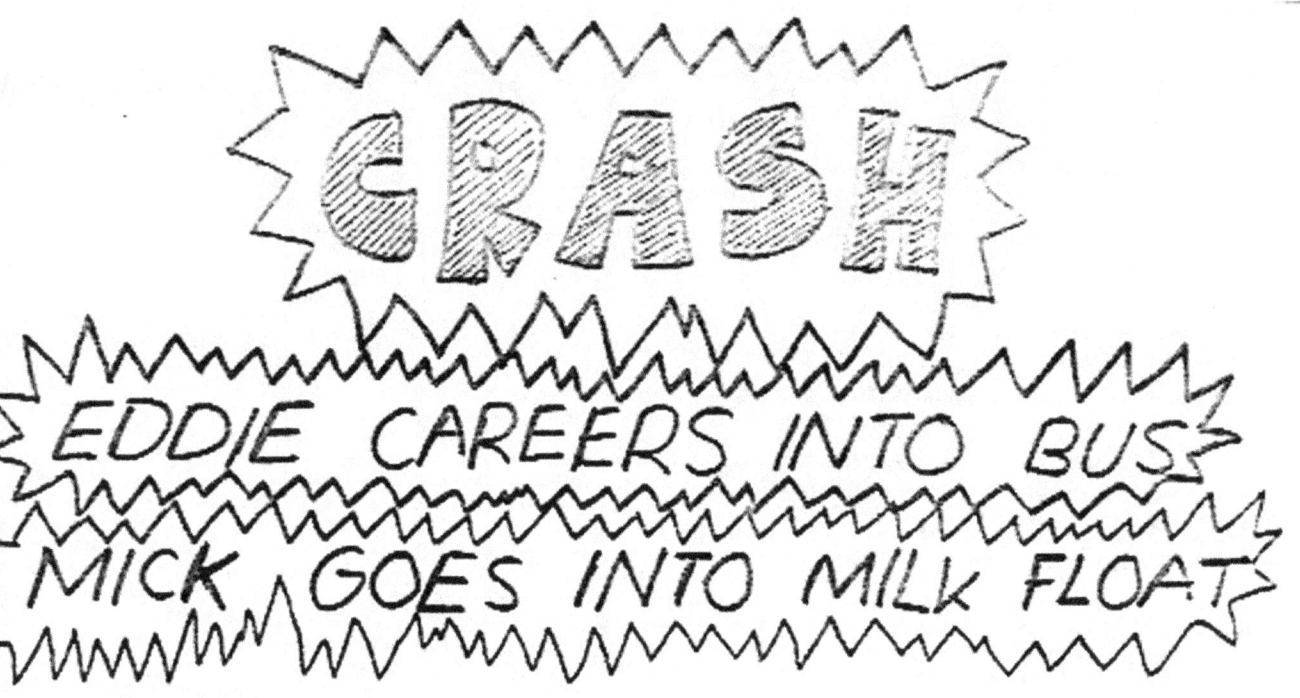

CRASH

EDDIE CAREERS INTO BUS

MICK GOES INTO MILK FLOAT

POLICE NOTICE

BEWARE: IF YOU SEE A SMALLISH, UGLY, BALD HEADED FIFTY YEAR OLD MAN IN A
BLUE CAVALIER STAY AWAY FROM HIM. DO NOT AND WE REPEAT DO NOT ENTER THIS
MANS CAR HE IS HIGHLY DANGEROUS. THIS INHUMAN BEING HAS BEEN KNOWN TO
DELIBRATLY CAREER INTO THE BACK OF STATIONARY BUSES. HE ESCAPES ARREST
BY CLAIMING THAT HIS EVER SHINING FORHEAD DAZZLES HIM FROM THE REFLECTION
OF HIS WING MIRROR. IF YOU SEE THIS MAN DO NOT APPROCH HIM HE IS HIGHLY DANGEROUS.

****

Well Eddie you're in a right mess this time arn'T you, police notices out,
the public very wary to travel by bus etc etc. You must look where you're
going in future instead of constantly dreaming of a revolutionry new hair replacer.

****

ALSO ON THE SUBJECT OF NASTY BASHES A RELIABLE SOURCE TOLD US THIS WEEK THAT
ALSO MICK BARNES HAD HAD A PRANG EARLER THIS YEAR (OR LATE LAST YEAR).
THIS HOWEVER WAS NO ORDINARY CRASH, IT SEEMS AS THOUGH MICK BARNES HAD PLANNED
THIS ONE OUT BEFORE HAND!

Raid on milk van,

JUST FOR THOSE OF YOU WHO
ARE THINKING THIS IS ALL
MADE UP WELL IT REALLY IS
TRUE, MICK BARNES REALLY
DID CRASH INTO A MILK VAN!

NEXT ISSUE MARK SHEPHER HITS MARS BAR TRUCK!

A POEM by Ashley Welburn

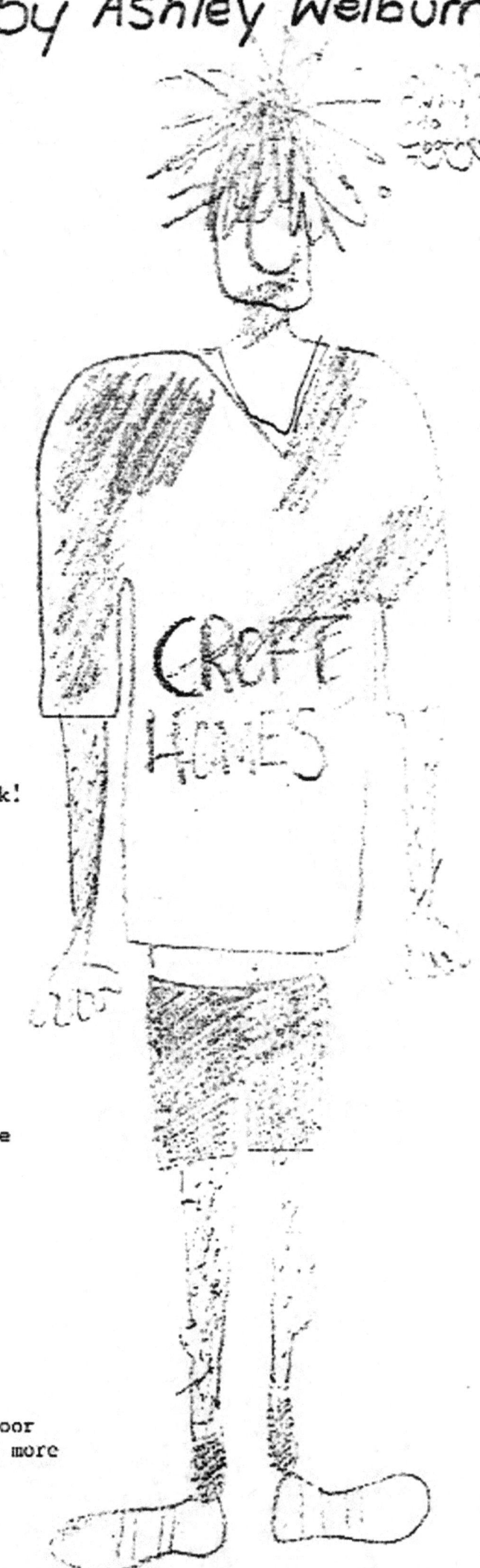

ODE TO GOAL SCORING

We all look forward to Saturday
To see the Dale come out and play
But there's a crisis looming up
Which will prevent us from winning a Cup

The problem's there for all to see
With talent we've got it's a mystery
The malady's bad as it can get
We can't seem to find the back of the net

Andy Johnson has the skill
He really should score at his will
But when his shots hit from afar
The keeper tips it over the bar

Lee looks confident and very neat
He's got a pair of dancing feet
He stops to take another glance
The keeper's grabbed it - what a chance!

Shep has gone up in attack
We really need to pull one back
We've got one here, it's in the bag
He's hit the bloody corner flag!

Andy's injury healed up quick
We've played West Pier twice, that's the trick!
His well struck shot is looking good
Oh deary me it's hit the wood!

It's good to see Glen back enjoying the fun
He's started on one of his mazey runs
Looks as though we'll score at last
The keeper's gone and turned it past!

I can't believe what I'm seeing here
Richard Bradley's in the clear
He's beaten the defensive wall
Well ****er me he's missed the ball

Sean's crunched through a tackle, and two more
He really looks about to score
This is why he's in the side
Well ****er me he's pulled it wide

One more to beat and looking good
Eddy will score, or so he should
But just as a chance is going to go in
He decides to kick his opponent's shin

The management's patience is wearing thin
They select a side which they hope will win
'Well!' says Barney as his brolly hits the floor
'I don't believe it!' says Ake as we miss two more

(continued on next page)

ODE TO GOAL SCORING (CONTINUED)

Baldo's up for a corner kick
He loves to be right in the thick
As the ball comes over to our dismay
He's headed it back the other way!

The supporters' patience is beginning to crack
It's time we had Vic and Brian back
Is Besty right? Are they all crap?
We must get Dale back on the map

Next match Ryedale - bloody hell!
They can't score a goal aswell!
'I never fail to score goals here'
Dicko's words ring loud and clear

Glen starts us off with a deflected shot
Which Denis the keeper could not have got
Then Dicko's prophecy comes true
He goes and scores the other two!

Now we're back on song again
We'll cause the others a lot of pain
We've rediscovered how to score
Here's to Dale scoring many more!

                    TAW

EDITORS NOTE: Thanks to our secretary there for a fantastic piece of poetry —
he will recieve a free copy of this issue for his efforts! We are looking for
other things written by players - anyone who gives us anything can have a free
copy...

****

DALE WIN

JUST TO PROVE TO THE DALE PLAYERS OR SUPPORTERS WHO DIDN'T TURN UP FOR THE RYEDALE
GAME THAT WE DID ACTUALLY WIN AND IT WASN'T A BIG LIE HERE IS THE GAZETTE AND
HERALD PAPER CUTTING TO PROVE IT:

The third division local derby at Ryedale Sports Club Reserves saw visitors Thornton-le-Dale put in a blistering first-half performance to win 3-0. Two early goals for Dale were scored by Glen Baskcyfield — his shot appeared to be deflected past Ryedale's impressive keeper, Dennis Smith — and Sean Dixon made it 2-0 in the early period of the game.

Dixon added a second goal before half-time. Ryedale did better in the second half with substitute, David Johnson, outstanding.

THE DALE DIDN'T EVEN LET
A GOAL IN!
WE STILL CAN'T BELIEVE IT

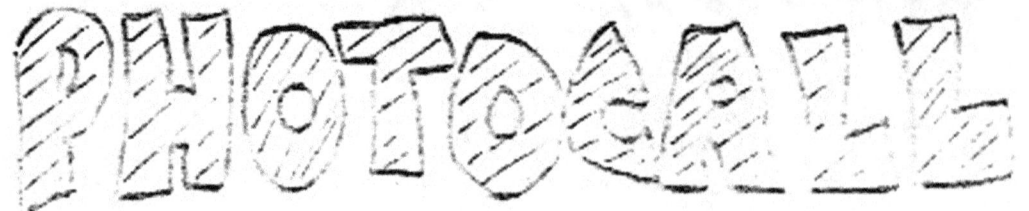

PHOTOCALL

MUCH AS WE'D LIKE TO PRINT A PHOTO OF NICK VERMONT WE ARE VERY
SORRY BUT HE HAS SEEMED TO HAVE DISAPPEARED!

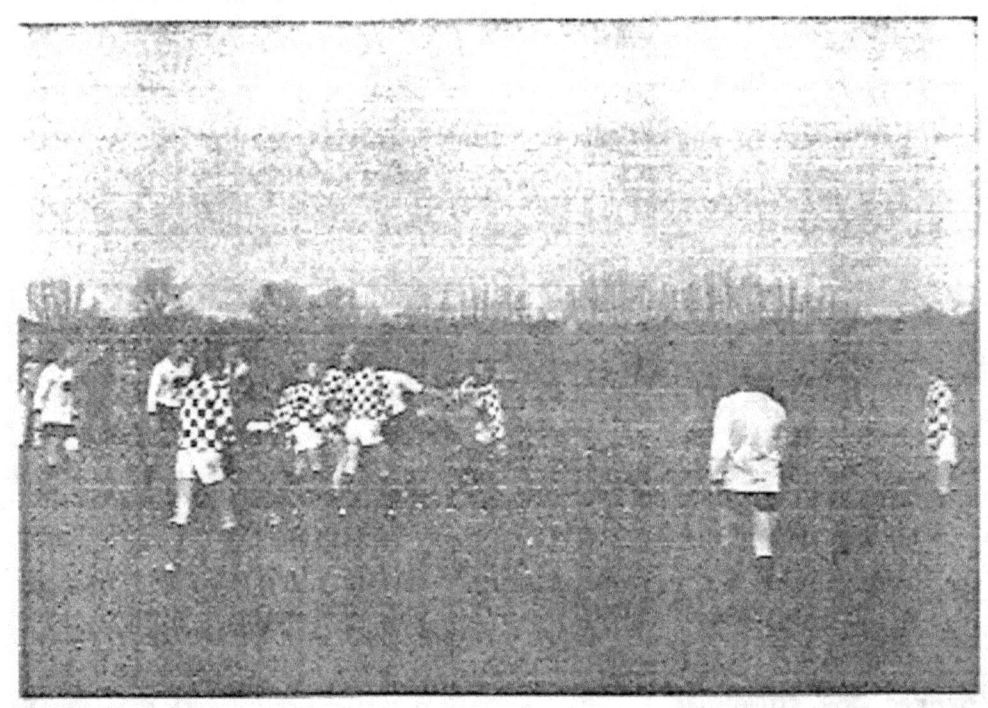

FIRST IAN BIGGINS WENT THEN STEVE AVISON, AS THE ABOVE PHOTO SHOWS
THESE MEN WERE HARD WHY DON'T WE HAVE MORE PLAYERS LIKE THESE?
By the way notice Besty in the background hurling abuse but keeping
arms length away.

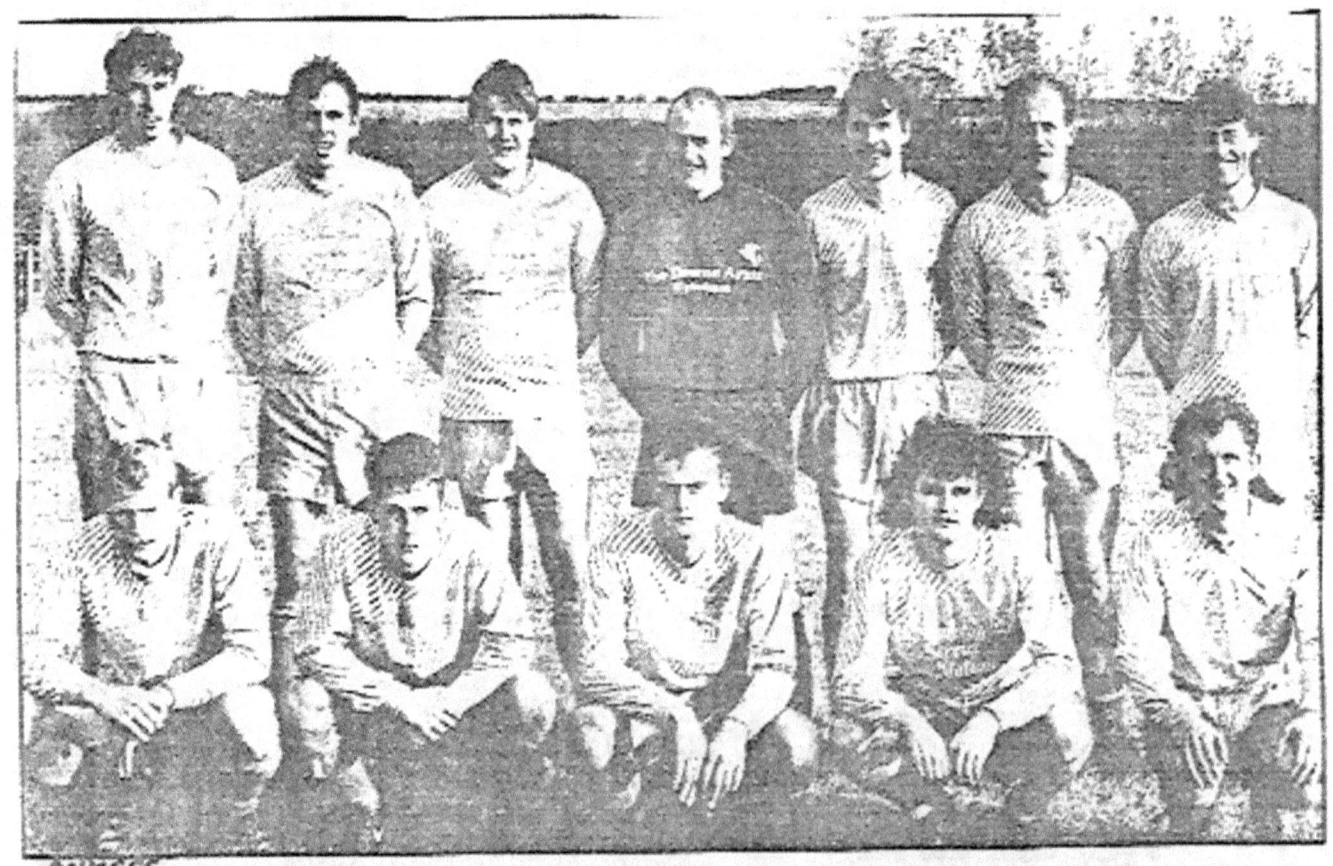

WORKSOP FC: Pictured from back left are B Best, C Robinson, A Wood, A Lakin, P Marston, T Martin, J
Agar, P Lakin, G Goodwin, R Ward, I Lambert and D Harrison

HERE HE IS AGAIN (BESTY) THIS TIME WITH HIS NEW FOUND UGLY SQUAD. Notice the keeper!

Hi ho ho. WHAT A BUNCH OF UGLY B******DS

BACK TO THE FUTURE

Recently, your riving editorial team came across a very sleek black porsche.
As the doors were unlocked, we got in and decided to go for a spin. After
pressing a few buttons, we whizzed 20 years into the future just like that youth
out of the film! So here we were stuck in the year 2010, all we could do was
write an insight on the Dale and wait to be struck by lightning...

We made our way up to the ground, bemused by the fact that so many cars were
whizzing past us and bewildered by the signs of 'GREYHOUND STADIUM - AHEAD'
which littered the roadside. Many of the passers-by had orange and black scarves
hanging out of the car windows and some were shouting 'Wolves is gonna get yer'
at us. Bloody hell, we thought, Wolves must have fallen on bad times recently.
How wrong we were. We attempted to climb the gate into the ground but were met
by a massive security fence. A copper told us to 'Go to turnstile 4A and you're
sure to get in.' This we did, amazed by the car parks that had sprung up and
by the massive plastic blob which stood before us. 'Another bloody factory'
muttered Steve, 'Where the f**k's our ground?'
Funnily enough we were ushered through into this monstrosity and saw a great 4-tier
stadium staring at us, a running track, it was twice as big as Wembley. 'Bloody
hell, have Liverpool moved house?' we thought, dumbstruck. An old gent heard
our comments and said, 'I know, it's amazing what that Mick Barnes did for us'.
I thought I'd better by a programme and approached a youth who looked suprisingly
familiar. Four quid for a programme these days! Disgraceful! On looking through
the advert filled glossy, we realised that this was Dale's first ever division 4
league game! We were sponsored by the multi-national company 'Croft Homes Inc'
who were pumping millions into the club, and apparently we had undergone a
remarkable turnaround during the 1990's, when during the 1990/1 season, Mike
Aconley was sacked. Since then we had rocketed through the leagues to meet
Wolves in our first ever div 4 game! So that was who the prog seller was, Shaun's
dad! We asked him where his son was at the moment. 'Still climbing trees and
playing with the girlies?' joked Steve. 'Ignorant b***ard' came the reply, 'He's
our tossin' centre forward!' We fainted but on regaining consciousness we noticed
a long haired youth trying to give us a filthy piece of paper. 'Escaped Horse'
he muttered, '50 ecu's'.
'Have we got that one?' I asked, to be told, 'It's the first week it's being sold,
number 10002 sold out!' We bought one and looked through the 100-odd pages
of brilliant humour, slagging off players and marvellousness. 'Ha, it hasn't
changed a bit!' We all agreed.
Well we gradually got used to all this glamour, were filled in on all the details
by a proud Mike Aconley, who informed us that Mick Barnes was still going strong
and that today would be the long awaited return of Vic Welburn, whose boots
had finally arrived. As the 'Kop' filled up, I said something I shouldn't
have. 'Where's Mermaid?' I enquired innocently. 10,000 faces turned to stare
at me. Shit. A while later Mike informed us that in 1994 during a game between
the two clubs Mermaid players pulled out hand grenades and machine guns and
shot all our players, luckily we all survived thanks to 'Karate Kid' Deggy Bond
and the fact that Mark Shepherd had sheltered the entire team by wrapping himself
around them. Mermaid had long since been disbanded. On the domestic scene, Leeds
had fallen on hard times, fighting amongst players and irregular payments along
with Gordon Strachan joining title contenders Wimbledon had meant that they
were in division 4 and would be playing us this year. Apparently last year
during a 6-0 home defeat by struggling Rochdale their most loyal fan Ralph
Ingleby had finally thrown his scarf away in disgust, pulled all his clothes
off and invaded the pitch. Leeds were now in financial turmoil with gates
rarely exceeding 600 and looked set to fold in the near future!
Mike stopped reminiscing now as the game started, Dale's first ever league moment
had arrived...

We stayed in the future for years, we will share our amazing experiences with you
season by season in all the future issues of 'Escaped Horse' beginning next
time with the season 2010/11

ESCAPED HORSE PROUD OFFICIALS

Well we've decided it's about time we ought to publish our list of Escaped Horse officals and associates. So below is the complete list. Don't be surprised if your name comes up, sorry if you don't like your role but remember not everyone can be an Escaped Horse offical!

CHAIRMAN- B.Best and anyone with money
DIRECTORS- This space will be left blank for the person who sends us the most money
EDITORIAL TEAM- P.Staniforth, M.Staniforth, S.Allerdice?
CONTRIBUTORS- B.Best, Brompton keeper, anyone who gives us a good story
PHOTO'S- P.Staniforth, M,Staniforth and the occasional one from Andy Thrill
ARTWORK- Editorial team
PROMOTION- ?
RESEARCH- Ed's again
EXCLUSIVE STORYS ABOUT SHEP- Barny, A.Thrill, Howard Jackson
AUSTRALIAN CONTINGENT- A.Thrill
OFFICAL ESCAPED HORSE STINGY B*****DS- R.Bradley, M.Shepherd (quote Mick Barnes)
OFFICAL ESCAPED HORSE HERO- V.Welburn
OFFICAL ESCAPED HORSE BIG DOGS COCK- J.Bevan
OEFICAL ESCAPED HORSE COMIC- Deggy Bond
OFFICAL ESCAPED HORSE MAD B*****DS- Anyone playing away at Hunmanby
OFFICAL ESCAPED HORSE WANKERS- Mermaid F.C
TEABOY- S.Allerdice
PUBLISHERS- MOORLANDS (bloody con)
INSPIRATION- God knows where!

Sorry if you haven't spotted your name here but send us some cash and you're sure to get in somewhere! Oh yes and one we nearly forgot- OFFICAL E.S POET- A.Welburn

****

MORE BUCK BRAWLS

Well it really looks like the Buck Inn in Thornton Dale is the place to be, more illustrious tales have been passed to us from some of the regulars....

SHEP IN CENSORED

JUST SO SHEP BUYS IT NEXT WEEK!

HILL, ANOTHER BIG DOGS COCK

This time the astonishing story below was brought to us by none other than A.Thrill. According to our Ossie contingent the Dales own goalkeeper Stuart Hill has also been in little scuffles in the pub. This story is quite vague but as we gather it, it sounds like our Stuart got into a little tussle after a yob, probably from Mermaid, called him 'a big soft red cock'. Schoolboy Julian Bevan was heard to say that he was very proud someone else had joined the club!

THE ESCAPED HORSE

DEDICATED TO QPR FANZINE 'OOH I THINK IT'S MY GROIN'

DALE SIGN UP ENTIRE NEW SQUAD!

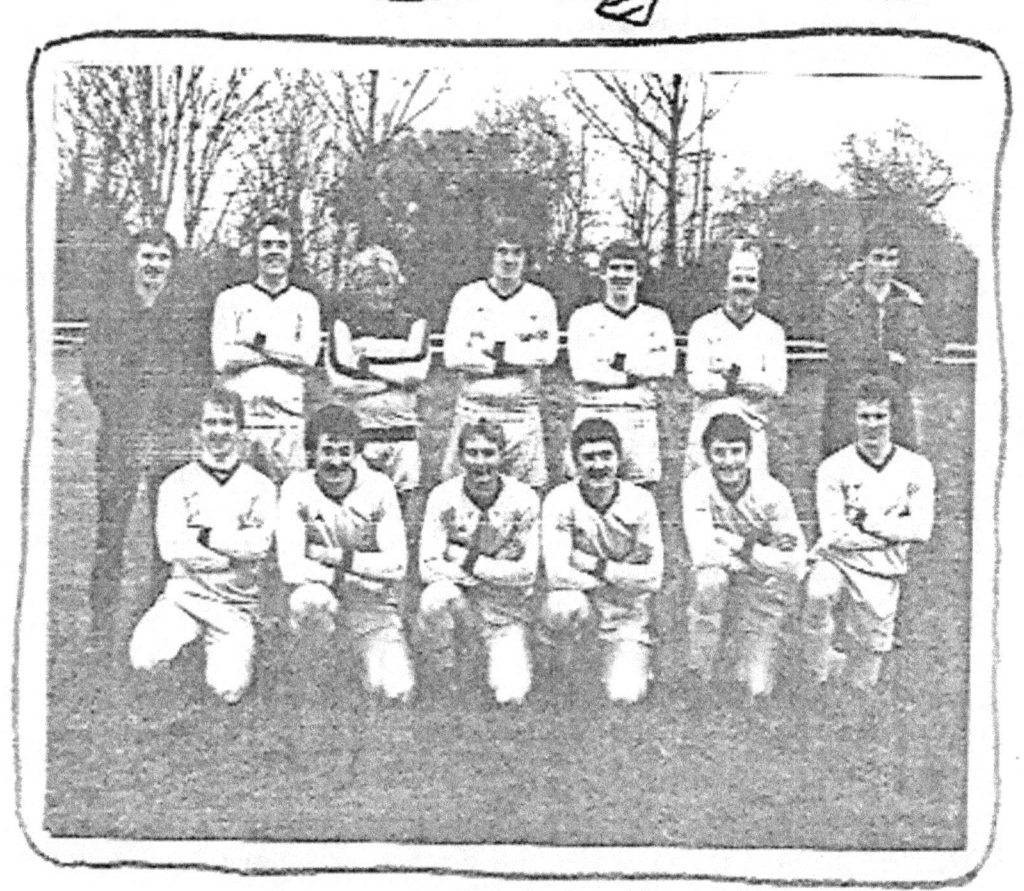

INSIDE - MORE EXCLUSIVE PHOTO'S, GREYHOUND GOSSIP, PLUS - FIND OUT HOW DALE'S SEASON IN THE YEAR 2010 WENT

Greyhound Grapevine

EDITORIAL
Back at last, we're really sorry you had to wait so long for this edition and we hope nobody was drawn to tears. Anyway we're back now so stop crying and read on. Bloody British weather, every single game was cancelled so we couldn't even go and take the piss out of Besty at Wykeham. We we're going to try and clear the snow off the pitch for last weeks game (honest) but he was just to deep. Going back a few weeks ago the E.S editorial team were very pleased about seeing the exciting return of the legendary Mike Aconley and hope that the alot better, supporters hero Victor Welburn we soon follow (take note management). Speaking about the management we had better win today or Mick Barnes must surely have to hand in his resignation and as we reveal in the next few pages Burney may go soon anyway. Before we leave you to read the amazing features inside we'd like to ask if anyone knows which one Eddie Avison is on the front cover, is he the one second from the right on the back row or is he the one first from the right on the front row?

ESCAPED HORSE TO BE IN PAPER?
Fame at last soon the subscriptions should be flocking in. Why we here you asking yourselves because according to Dean Richardson (Dales super sub) we could be reviewed in one of the local papers! Dean informed us that writer for the Gazette Keith Sales asked him to get a few copies of the best fanzine in England so he could write about them. We at the Escaped Horse havn't heard anything from the man yet but hopefully Dean is telling the truth and the village of Thornton Dale will be put on the map! Also our friend Dean did an interview for us which was meant for this issue but he hasn't given it back to us yet

BRADLEY IS VALENTINE
Another exclusive from the Escaped Horse is revealed here. It seems that Richard 'left in Garbuts' Bradley has a secret admirer and he hasn't told anyone about it. Whilst poor old Shep and Andy Thrill sat all depressed at not getting any cards on Valentines day Bradders was laughing he got at least one and only the Escaped Horse know who it was from, no names will be printed (unless you give us endless amounts of money) but we will say Andy Thrill may be quite yealous (it wasn't the ozzies!).

BALDERSONS PART TWO
Printed in the last edition was an article slagging off Baldersons cafe but it turns out that everything said was not quite true. Again last week two bedraggled reporters were staving and hungary with nowhere to go. The only place open was the one and only Baldersons bread shop. It was a big risk but the lads ventured in. Believe it or not it actually wasn't too bad and they did have a bit more than very old mince pies! The sausage rolls were really quite nice, or was it all a lovely(?) dream?

HILL IN HULL
There was rumours going round about something to do with Andy Thrill and Mark Shepherd in a Hull night club but we are not quite sure what this one was about, will someone please inform us.

QUOTES OF THE WEEK
Eddie Avison- "Wheres all me hair gone", after seeing this weeks cover

Eddie Avison- "Who needs a tracksuit when you've got a boiler suit"

Richard Bradley- "Thirty pence,bloody 'ell"

THANKS TO
Arsenal, for beating Leeds
Norwich , for beating Man Utd
Moorlands, especcially the nice lady who
does the photocopying

NO THANKS TO
Mermaid
Wykeham
Baldersons, for taking
over the corner cafe
The bloody weather
Iraq

From the ARCHIVES

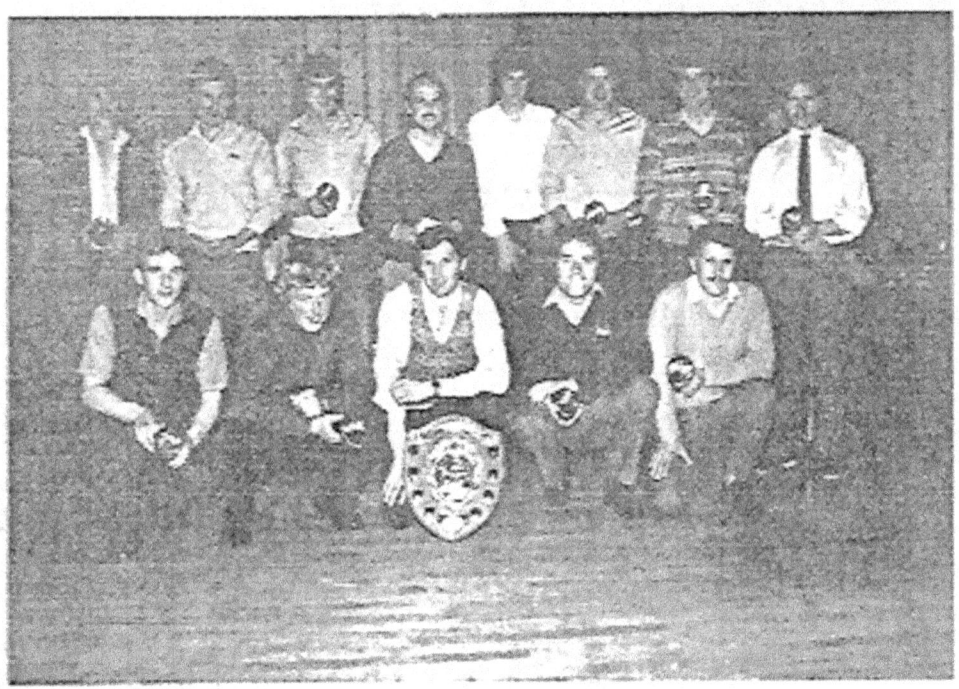

As if the front cover isn't enough, we've got another exclusive pic from the TDFC reference library! Rumoured to have been photogrpahed around 1983, there are some real cuties amongst this lot! How about Raymond Smith's fashion sense? (Back row, far left) Stuart Hill's lovely pink cheeks and sensationally, Eddie Avison's head! Has he been rolling in a mud bath or is it hair we can see!

Flicking back to the front cover and look closely at Mick Barnes' and Mike Aconley's stomachs! You were even fatter in them days Barney! Shades of Mark Shepherd? Stuart Hill has those lovely red cheeks still and we just adore Eddie Geary's white tights! And no, your eyes are not playing up, there's Eddie with that full head of hair again! Those were the days...

****

Next issue's 'From the archives' will concentrate on the season when Dale were in the same league as Scarborough FC (Yes, it's true).......................

****

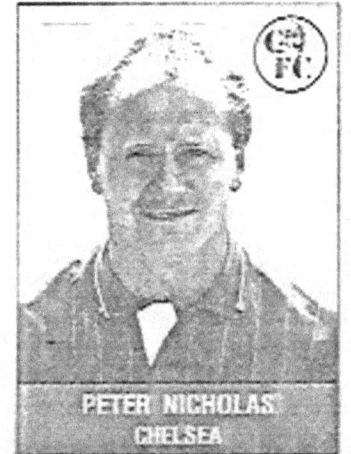

PETER NICHOLAS
CHELSEA

NUMBER ONE IN A SERIES OF ONE:

Players on Panini stickers who look remarkably like Eddie Avison.

Number 1: Peter Nicholas (Chelsea)

Or has this youth got a bit too much?

Dale's Subbuteo Team

came across the subbuteo items below in a sports shop
ote the startling resemblance to members of Dale's squad

ART HILL   MARK SHEPHERD   RAYMONDSMITH   EDDIE AVISON
↓   ↓   ↓ a hill   ↓ (It has nothing
                              (he is over   on top!)
                               it)

****

ANOTHER SENSATIONAL NEW SERIES FROM THE ESCAPED HORSE: WE PROUDLY PRESENT:

GREAT WEST HAM AND CHELSEA GIBBINGS OF OUR TIME

Yes folks, we've found the ideal way to take the piss out of those two young
upstarts, Julian Bevan and Lee Brackstone. Julian is a demented Chelsea fan
while Lee and we are informed, his dad, are members of the 'Claret and Blue
army.' So every issue we will publish details of great gubbings these teams
have suffered over the years. Therefore when either of the lads slag you off
in future just reply with, 'Scarborough 3 Chelsea 2, October 1989' etc. That
will soon shut them up. So, here's this weeks selection to make the laddies
angry...

                    Wolves 8 Chelsea 1   September 1953

                    Blackburn 8 West Ham 2   December 1963

Ho ho, more next time folks but remember to keep reminding them of those scores!
By the way an absolutely hilarious story we've just remembered which we must
tell you about Julian. (We guarantee it is true, honestly!)
When Scarborough were drawn with Chelsea in October 1989 Littlewoods Cup tie,
Jules could not believe his luck. He'd just moved house from London or somewhere
and now could see his favourites in action at Scarborough! However, Julian could
not get a ticket for the Chelsea section so he went into the Scarborough end
of the ground! Julian was making some smiles to himself when the Londoners
went 2-0 up but then Scarborough came back to score twice and make it 2-2.
Away goals were still in Chelsea's favour but then Boro got a penalty which they
scored. The fans went mental (Well I did at least) and to avoid looking too
obvious Julian was forced to cheer and clap with the rest of us as Chelsea were
getting pissed on!

****

SOME BLOODY USELESS FACTS ABOUT ANDY JOHNSON

1. Andy Johnson looks like a drug addict.
2. Andy Johnson is meant to have written a book.
3. Andy Johnson likes the Carpenters.
4. Andy Johnson is going to dub a 'Waterboys' cassette for Andy Thrill.
5. Andy Johnson rode in the passenger seat of Mick Barnes' car on the way back
from Scalby.
6. Andy Johnson always seems to be injured.
7. Andy Johnson buys 'When Saturday Comes'.
****

ANDY SHARES HIS THRILLS

Ex Dale favourite Andy Thrill has been at it again, out on the bird pull and
the Escaped Horse have got all the inside infomation on it given to us by none
other than the lucky/unlucky girl herself. We refused not to print anything
about this as she wanted but we won't reveal any names just yet. The lucky
lady quoted to the Escaped Horse that she didn't want anything printed because
"I don't want it to spoil our relationship". According to the nameless girl
she was putting beer mats down the poor lads jumper in the Buck(of course)
and Thrill wasn't actually refusing this. Also there was rumours that Thrill
had asked her out but she claims they are untrue.We are hoping Andy won't get
to upset about us prying into his private life but she sees him as fun loving
so we don't think he will. She also claims him to be shy, shy bollocks this
mans had more women than there are soldiers in the bloody Gulf. Also by the
way Thrill's ex P.E teacher claimed a few weeks back that he was always moody
at school, a side she has yet to see. Hopefully we'll have a photo of Andys
true love next week so watch this space.

****

BEER GLASS SAGA CONTINUED o o o

Again this story was given to us by Andy Thrills lucky girl who also gave us
the above (well actually she didn't but we must blame it on someone for when
Shep gets raged). After hearing last issue about Eddie Avisons prang into a
bus and Mick Barnes crash into a milk float you will be shocked to hear there
has been another car war. According to a source we cannot reveal Mark Shepherd
ran into a truck full of beer glasses just outside Thornton Dale. The funny
thing about this story was that as the glassea shattered everywhere hundreds
of little green aliens ran out of the truck! Could someone give us a bit more
info on this one please. You'll have to be a regular of the Buck to understand
this one and if not see issue nine on the back page. Sorry Mark returned by
popular demand.

****

BARNES FOR LIVERPOOL?

Shock news in just before we went to press. Soon after Mick Barnes was in a
management scandle with Scalby it turns out the veteran may take his skills
to none other than first division Liverpool. After Barnes heard that Dalglish
had resigned from the great club we were told by a nameless contact that he
was already having talks with Liverpool. The reason that Dalglish resigned
we were told was because his place was under constant threat from the Dale
manager. We also heard rumours that Barney may secretly get the job of manager
at rivals Everton and it all sounds a bit suspect to us. We're sure we've
heard this one before. Hopefully more info will be given next issue and there
maybe even an exclusive interview with the Thornton/Scalby/Liverpool/Everton
manager.

****

BACK TO THE FUTURE

This sensational peep into the future has been written after your editors
made an unbelieveable journey to the year 2010. For full details, see the last
edition. If you hadn't bought it, then it's your own fault.
This is Dale's first season in division 4 and with crowds now around 15,000
3 new stands have been built.
Our first game at home v Wolves saw a large visiting support, some of whom climbed
on to the stands and fell through the roof! We had told Barney to get it fixed
but it turned out ok! Anyway, Shaun Aconley scored our first league goal before
a great one-two between Steve and Craig Barnes set up number 2 for a youthful
Victor Welburn. We were shocked at half time when instead of the usual sexy fillies
carrying goal-den goal numbers round on a board, it was Deggy Bond in a leotard!
After the 2-0 win we went to Leeds but were met by a swimming pool! Demented fan
Ralph Ingleby, who had seen his team fall on half times in recent years, explained
that they had decided to play under water because they had heard there were 20,000
leagues under the sea, so they must have a good chance of winning one of them!

It was here we picked up a copy of the Escaped Horse, number 10005. Inside we saw
a 'Craig Barnes sex scandal' and 'Victor Welburn gets new boots' shock exclusive.
Only 300 Leeds fans bothered to turn up and see Dale's second win, by 1-0.
Our next game was postponed at Scarborough because of snow. Directors had appealed
for fans to clear the pitch, but only one had turned up! Fans were in uproar
after the amangement snapped up ageing John Barnes from cash starved Liverpool
for £5million, many thought it was a waste of money. An FA Cup run was not on the
cards after being drawn at league leaders QPR, winner of the league for 10 seasons
and unbeaten for three years, although we put up a brave fight to only go down 65-0
(You'll have to review it now, eh?)

Besty meanwhile was making millions this week with a modern housing project in
windswept Hunmanby, he had sponsored the League Cup, a competition which saw
us fall 3-1 at Ipswich in the first round. Ashley Welburn had become a world
famous poet and Eddie Avison was a bus driver! By Christmas we were in 4th
place, still without conceding any goals because 50 stone keeper Mark Shepherd
was impossible to beat. Iraq by now had invaded the Faroe Islands after the tiny
country beat them 1-0 in a supposed friendly.

After an incredibly boring 3 months we were in the play offs with a game against
Leeds barring our progress to the 3rd division. Would we make it? Tune in next
time to find out, what a load of shite we've just written. By the way, here are
the honours lists for season 2010/11:

DIVISION 1 CHAMPIONS   - QUEENS PARK RANGERS
DIVISION 2 CHAMPIONS - CANTON RESERVES
DIVISION 3 CHAMPIONS   - DUBLIN CITY
DIVISION 4 CHAMPIONS - SCARBOROUGH LADIES
SCOTTISH PREMIER - EAST STIRLING
DIVISION 1 - ALBTON ROVERS
DIVISION 2- RANGERS (minus Graeme Souness)
GM VAUXHALL CONF - HEMEL HEMPSTEAD
MANCHESTER SUNDAY LEAGUE DIVISION 33 - MANCHESTER UNITED

PS - All the time we've been writing this, Gillingham v Halifax has been on the
radio. It was a pulsating game with Gillingham snatching it at the death.
Just thought you'd like to know...

THE BACK PAGE

COMIC RELIEF

Well as March the fiftenth draws nearer Dale players have been deciding what to do for their contributions to Comic Relief. Here is afew of the antics some of the players will be getting up to:

EDDIE AVISON-sponsored head shave
RICHARD BRADLEY-sponsored sit in, in Garbuts
MICK BARNES-sponsored sit in, in the pub
MARK SHEPHERD-guess what
ANDY JOHNSON-sponsored freeze at Hunmanby

As well as these Brian Best will be staging the first ever 'try and hit the corner flag' competition and Mermaid will be holding a sponsored riot in Bridlington (no doubt Ian Biggins and Steve Avison will be there).

Also so the Escaped Horse do there part in the fun we print the below advertisment

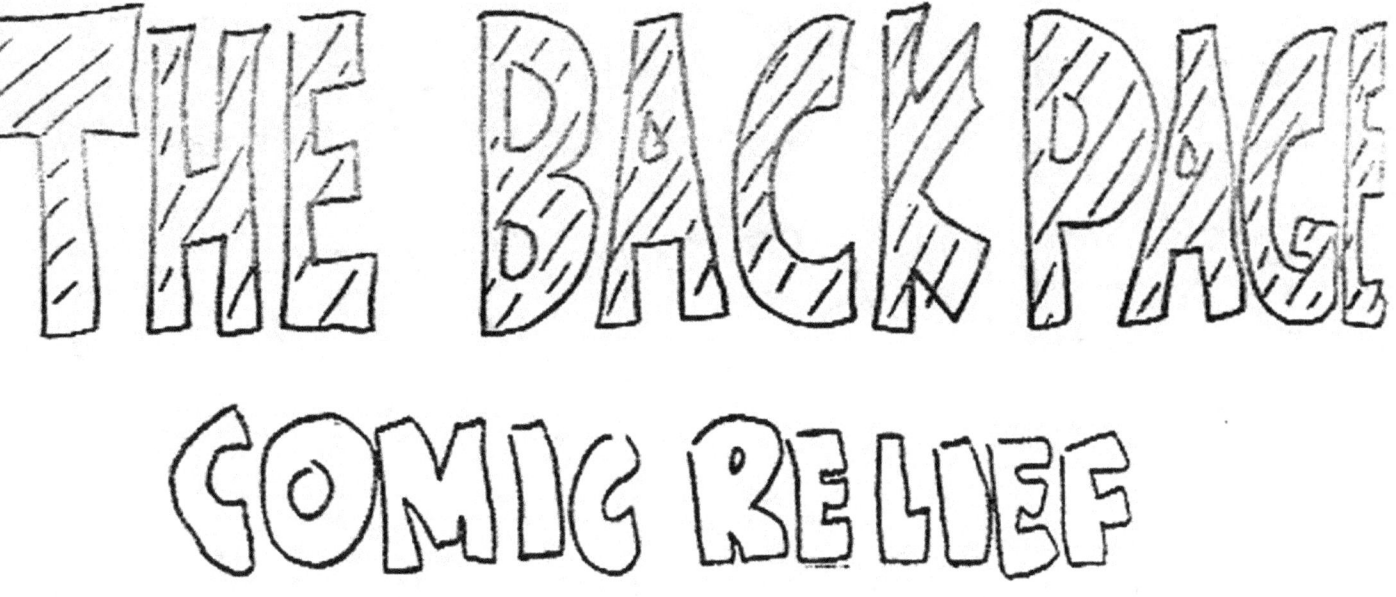

ANDY HILL RED CONKS!

ONLY £1·00 FROM THE ESCAPED HORSE

TWICE THE SIZE FOR ONLY 40p MORE!

****

A special mention this week goes out this week to Richard 'Garbuts' Bradley who actually bought a funzine last time. This was a very emotional event for the Escaped Horse as we realise Richard has come to his senses at last

Also Shaun Dixon just has to get a mention for his throw ins at Northcliff, very entertaining! Bye

RUBBLE HELPS SCALBY YOBS

When we reported a few issues ago that Mick Barnes was to sign for Scalby many Dale fans thought we were joking. So did we. However this startling story appears to now be true after our recent defeat at the hands of the Scarborough side. It appears that Mick the milk float had an agreement with the Scalby team beforehand that for a large amount of hard cash he would secretly pass on information about the Dale's strengths (?) and weaknesses. Obviously this sensational doing by Mr Rubble helped Scalby to slam two late goals past us. Who else would have told Scalby that they had to kick Bradders and Jono off the park to stand a chance of winning? All the clues point to one culprit. This must be the last nail in the coffin for Barney and he is now under increasing pressure from some sections of the Dale's legion of followers to resign.

****

ACONLEY TO TAKE PLACE OF THRILL

When Andy Thrill departed from this hallowed turf (?) a few weeks ago, your reporters were depressed to say the least. Who else could we take the piss out of? However, this apparent catastrophe turned into joy when we realised just who would be stepping into Thrill's shoes. Yes, after an absence of 30 odd years, Mike Aconley is back. And back with a bang, too. A sensational display on Ollie's Mount against North Cliff almost saw the return of those 'Mike Aconley Specials'. Alas not this week, but 'Ake' was obviously proud of his performance whispering afterwards that 'Bah gum, it brings back t'memories o' t' nineteen twenties'. Mike's sudden return was abruptly halted at the Scalby fiaco when cheat Mick Barnes, realising the danger this cult figure posed, dropped him! Obviously with the 'Escaped Horse' now a worldwide publication we have received multitudes of fan letters. One, produced in mysteriously familiar handwriting, read, 'I am an avid fan of the legendary Mike Aconley and am in desperate need of his autograph! I thought he had passed away years ago! Please send me his address or I will have to do something very drastic, like signing for Wykeham! yours sincerely, Brian West.'

In the third division, Thornton-le-Dale visited North Cliff at Oliver's Mount. Sean Dixon put the Dale into an early lead. On the stroke of half time North Cliff equalised and early in the second half they took the lead.

Willy Balderson equalised for the Dale, but North Cliff regained the lead after 75 minutes. In the last minute the impressive Mike Aconley burst forward for the Dale but his shot went narrowly wide of the target.

↖ WHO WRITES THIS CRAP ANYWAY?

DALE v BROMPTON

AN 'ESCAPED HORSE' PUBLICATION

EDITORIAL: So today it's time to meet our big rivals, the Brompton scummers, Kojak, crap 'Keeper and all. This is a special edition as our next issue is scheduled for next week and we couldn't resist slagging the ground-less tossers off! The next issue includes a sensational Stuart Hill shocker. This issue is dedicated to everyone who's bought the fanzine in the past and to those who don't usually buy it - don't complain if you haven't been given this one FREE!

****

A POEM

It's Dale v Brompton
We'll make such a sound
Even if they win
We've still got a ground

They share with Wykeham
They can't play the game
Each team plays crap
They're exactly the same

****

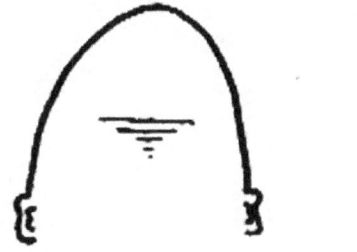

THE BROMPTON MANAGER'S
FOREHEAD

****

* TEAM NEWS

* Thanks to a strangely anonymous Brompton player who
* sent us a grubby little piece of paper with team
* news on, (and a page three from the Sun!) we can
* give you an insight into the visitors' squad for
* today's game:
*
* THE LETTER GOES AS FOLLOWS:
* Thought as the official 'Escaped Horse mole' in the
* BFC camp I'd drop you some team sheets for Saturday's
* big game. Please keep my identity secret (Alright if
* you say so Dave ! - Eds) otherwise no more inside info
* for you. Also I thought you could use some clippings
* from the enclosed tabloid page. (These will probably
* appear in our next issue - Eds)
*   yours,
*   Anon.
* The team is as follows: B.Manson, S.Scott, P.Lang,
* Dick Schnieder, 'Bonka'Hanby (Old Dale star pictured
* in issue 11), D.Hepplestone, 'Exocet' Newton, Martin
* 'I used to score when I played for Ryedale' Cook,
* Awesome Wells, Ian 'New signing' Warwick, Wass

DALE PEN-PICTURES

STUART HILL: Sheep shagging goalkeeper whose penalties are as lethal as Andy Thrill's nose.

MARK 'GAZZA SHEPHERD: We think you know what we were going to write so we'll leave it to your own imagination!

EDDIE AVISON: Player who bears a striking resemblance to the Brompton manager!

MICK BARNES: Prolific goalscorer who is built like a 'Brick shithouse'.

MIKE ACONLEY: Sorry, wrong year!

NICK VERMONT: Who?

VICTOR WELBURN: Amazing, brilliant, ace, God-like, heavenly, sensational, prolific, staggering, messiah, saviour, hero, when his boots have come!

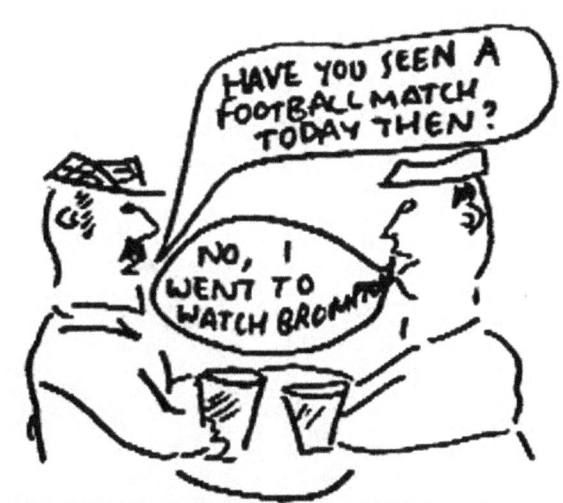

****

THANKS TO: Everyone who has bought the fanzine before, Dave H********* for the Brompton article, Whitby Arcadians for stuffing Wykeham, Moorlands.

NO THANKS TO: Richard Bradley for never buying the fanzine, Mick Barnes' letterbox, Mermaid FC, and of course Brompton.

****

FAMOUS DEGGY BOND QUOTES OF OUR TIME:
(On the way back from a Scarborough game after hearing result again on radio:

ISSUE 12   Even though we're in a recession it's still only 30p

THE ESCAPED HORSE

KICKING OFF WITH A
WORLD EXCLUSIVE TO
STUN TDFC:

EXPOSED:

STUART HILL'S SECRET COMPANY

Revealed: Advert in
'Sunday Sport' - 24 Feb 1991

ALSO INSIDE :-

3 EXCLUSIVE INTERVIEWS

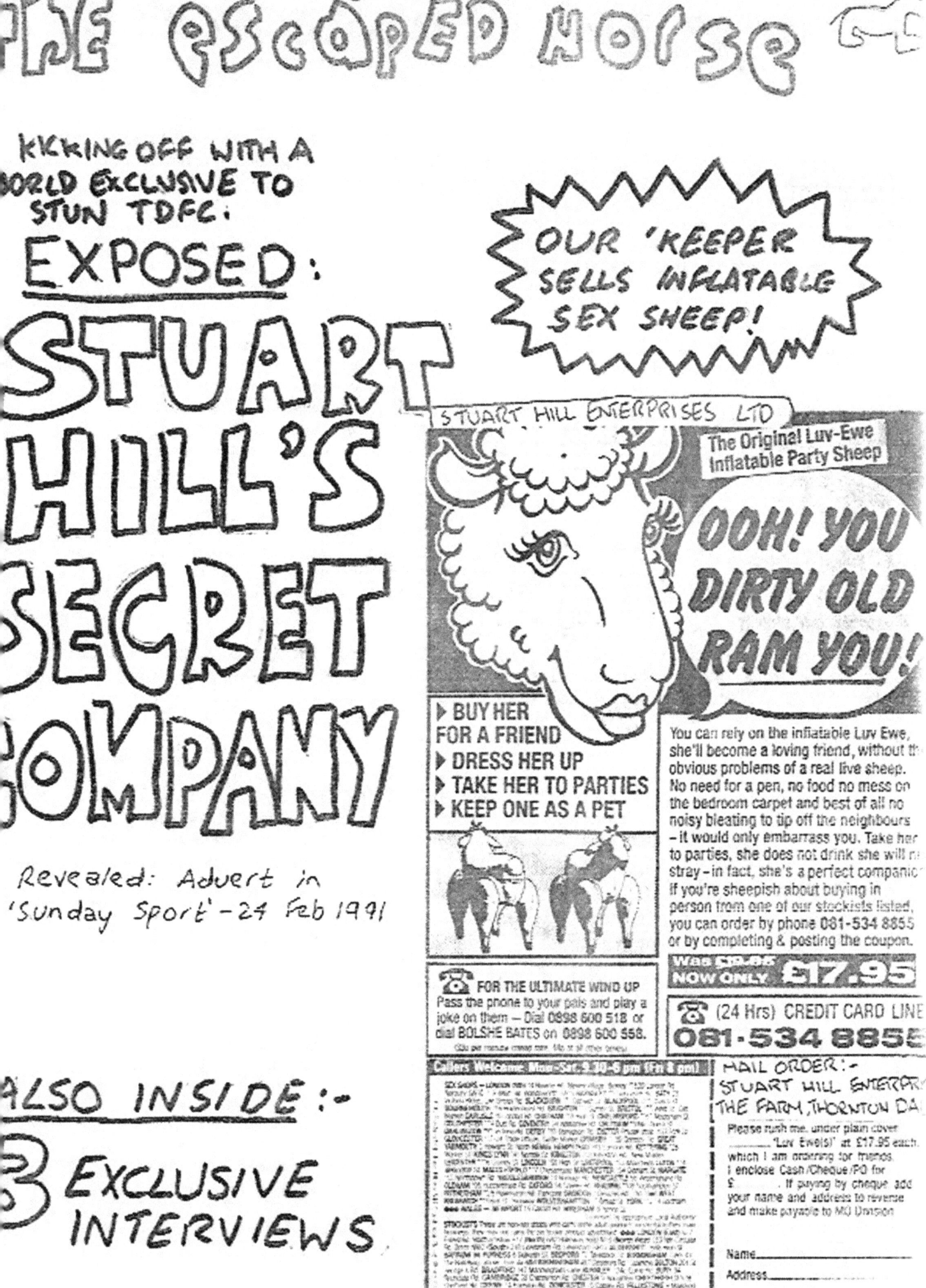

OUR 'KEEPER SELLS INFLATABLE SEX SHEEP!

STUART HILL ENTERPRISES LTD

The Original Luv-Ewe
Inflatable Party Sheep

OOH! YOU DIRTY OLD RAM YOU!

▶ BUY HER FOR A FRIEND
▶ DRESS HER UP
▶ TAKE HER TO PARTIES
▶ KEEP ONE AS A PET

You can rely on the inflatable Luv Ewe, she'll become a loving friend, without the obvious problems of a real live sheep. No need for a pen, no food no mess on the bedroom carpet and best of all no noisy bleating to tip off the neighbours – it would only embarrass you. Take her to parties, she does not drink she will not stray – in fact, she's a perfect companion. If you're sheepish about buying in person from one of our stockists listed, you can order by phone 081-534 8855 or by completing & posting the coupon.

Was ~~£19.95~~ NOW ONLY £17.95

☎ FOR THE ULTIMATE WIND UP
Pass the phone to your pals and play a joke on them – Dial 0898 600 518 or dial BOLSHE BATES on 0898 600 558.

☎ (24 Hrs) CREDIT CARD LINE
081-534 8855

MAIL ORDER :-
STUART HILL ENTERPR.
THE FARM, THORNTON DA

Please rush me, under plain cover
.... 'Luv Ewe(s)' at £17.95 each,
which I am ordering for friends.
I enclose Cash/Cheque/PO for
£.......... If paying by cheque add
your name and address to reverse
and make payable to MO Division

Name..........
Address..........
....
....
Postcode..........

Greyhound Grapevine

EDITORIAL.
We'll start this issue by saying that the Scarborough and District Football league
Association are a bunch of big dogs cocks for not giving us a game for weeks.
We don't even know if we'll be selling this issue on the touchline or in the pub
yet! Next we'd like to ask what the hell went wrong at Filey and why we only had
nine men? Anyway to make up for the misery of the last few weeks we've got a
bloody good issue out. Theres some amazing true exclusives in this issue, with
another Besty letter, three sensational interviews, a Stuart Hill shocker and
loads of other hot shit!

WHERES FILEY?
We don't really want to blame anyone for this but it really is a bit stupid if
we carn't even travel to Filey without losing three players along the way.
It seems as though last week Lee, Dean and Julian didn't turn up to the the
Filey away game. The Brackstones went to pick Dean up and were meant to follow
Barney to Filey. Barney says he beeped for them they don't seem to think so.
Julian did turn up at half time but the others didn't. Surely it's not that hard
to find your way to Filey.

JOHNSON PLAYS FOR WYKEHAM
We had it revealed to us a little while back that Andy Johnson went to a Wykeham
training session at the start of the season! Is the world falling apart? what
is this man playing at. If anyone else is having similar ideas we'd like to say
once and for all 'WYKEHAM ARE CRAP'. Don't do it for your own sake.

ASHLEY WELBURN PART TWO
Recently we've heard that someone else is to follow in the footsteps of the legendary
poet Ashley Welburn. Mick Barnes tells us that none other than ex Wykeham star
Andy Johnson has written us a world class piece of rhyming writing. Also Barnes
tells us that Andy won't submit it. What are you waiting for send it in and you'll
get a free copy!

GLENN READS THE HORSE AT WORK
It seems like The Escaped Horse cannot be put down as it is so good. Dale players
have even been spotted with them at work. Yes it's true Glenn Baskerfield even
takes his treasured copys to work with him. Glenn was spotted by an Escaped Horse
contingent while on a work experience interview at HPE Printers in Pickering!
Next we'll catch Andy Thrill reading one up his ladder!

AVISONS DRESS SENSE PULLS BIRDS!
According to an Escaped Horse source (we think it was Mark Shepherd) Andy Thrill
borrowed someones jumper to pull a bird. This in itself is quite a shocker,as
we all thought Thrill was attracted to his own sex, but this is not the main story
as the lovely jumper belonged to the one and only Eddie 'bald' Avison! Yes you
did read that right Eddie Avison! and according to our source the jumper had a
picture of Val Doonagan on it, the irish folk singer! Like we said earlier on,
is the world falling apart or is everyone else just out of touch with the fashion
world?

HILL IN TIFF WITH EX WYKEHAM STAR
We now have the reason why Andy Thrill stopped playing for Thornton. Here at E.S
we've heard that Thrill had a little tiff with Andy Johnson and because of this
stopped playing for the Dale! Could someone inform us a bit more here please.

QUOTES OF THE WEEK
Lee Brackstone- "Dean carn't take his ale"
Brian Best- "Scum"
Victor 'bloody good' Welburn- "Besty scored two, bloody hell"

SORRY IT'S MORE OF... BESTY'S LETTERS

These letters from Wykeham's saviour Brian Best just keep flooding in to the 'Escaped Horse' offices. The most recent one came with two photo's which are reproduced in the fanzine. So, here goes...

Dear Eds,

Please find enclosed two items of interest to any die hard Dale fans. Discovered at last the real reason behind many a Dale performance without bite! (but a load of foul play) as for the pedigree, it's my guess they're all mongrels! This also explains why many Dale players carry the alias of Dog Cock etc.

Also uncovered the bunker where many a made up article is conceived for the Dale fanzine, surely Eds with the mega donations and tee price of your editions could at least buy some paint.

Second thoughts it's as well the office blends with the hedgeback giving you all the cover available as more and more irate players seek the heads of their torments.

Please please don't despair with these rat infested quarters one day I am sure your talent will help you make the trip 8 miles due east of your present location to find real civilisation and quality to report on.
Find enclosed more silver for latest issues and a one way ticket.

                                    Besty

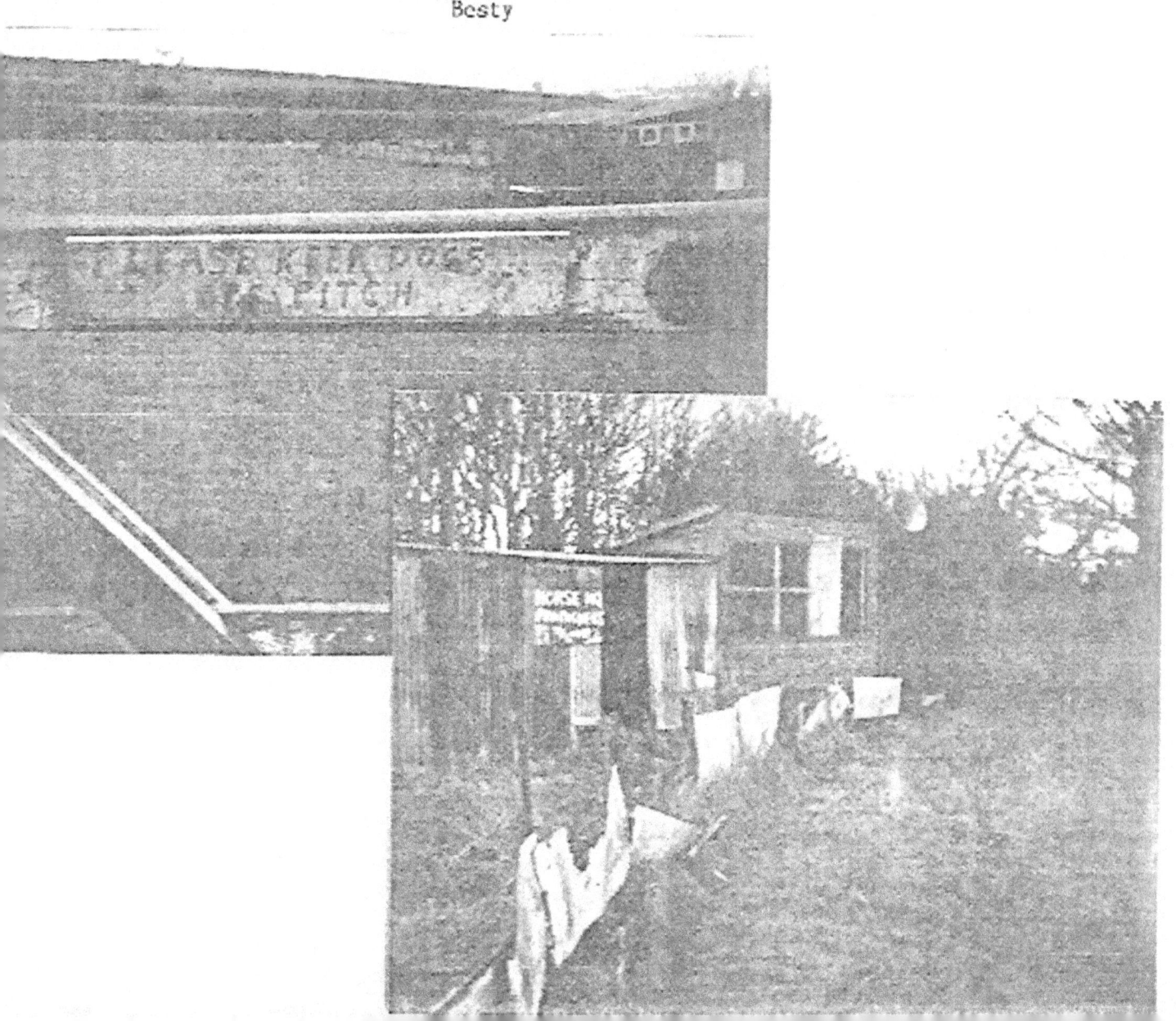

Well, it had to come sooner or later didn't it. When we sent Mr Thrill this question
sheet we did it in hope rather than anticipation, as we honestly didn't believe
Andy could read , let alone write. Which makes all this shite you are about to
read all the more amazing. His friends at the chip shop probably did it for him...

```
AGE:        21
FULL NAME:  Andrew Philip Hill
IS IT TRUE YOU'VE TOTALLY STOPPED PLAYING FOR TDFC?
            Hasn't everybody
WHAT'S ALL THIS ABOUT CRICKET AT LEEDS?
            Total fabrication
WHAT DO YOU THINK ABOUT TDFC?
            A sleeping dwarf
WHAT ABOUT THE MANAGEMENT?
            The Dale have management?
WHAT DO YOU THINK OF THE ESCAPED HORSE?
            Bollocks (you buy it-Eds)
IS IT TRUE YOU HAVE YOUR OWN 0898 LINE?
            No (blatant lie-Eds)
IS SHEP FAT?
            Is Mike Scott God!
COMMENTS ON BRIAN BEST:
            Oh you're crap you (B.D.C.2)
WHAT DO YOU THINK OF THE DALES FANS?
            Down and out wankers (you don't get a free issue-Eds)
IS IT TRUE THAT YOU'RE STARTING WORK IN THE CHIP SHOP?
            No comment
DO YOU KNOW ANYONE WITH THE INITIALS H.O?
            No comment
WHO ARE YOUR HEROES?
            Littlewoods man with big cheque, Kevin Turd Hird
WHO'S BEST ABBA OR THE WATERBOYS?
            Get real soft lads
IS YOUR NOSE TO LONG?
            No comment
WAS AUSTRALIA NICE?
            You are getting confused with a French town
IS VIC WELBURN BETTER THAN MIKE ACONLEY?
            At what?
WHERE WILL DALE FINISH THIS YEAR?
            Nowhere as per usual
FINAL COMMENTS:Piss off and die
```

This interview then concludes with Thrill drawing a shit picture of something
to do with The Waterboys. What a wanker!

..***

WE'D JUST THOUGHT THAT WE'D BETTER
PRINT THIS SO THAT THE LEGENDARY
GEORGE 'very bias' REIVLEY CAN PULL
OUT OF RETIREMENT AND COME BACK AND
HELP THE DALE IN THEIR STRUGGLE TO
GAIN PROMOTION TO DIVISION TWO NEXT
SEASON. WE HOPE OUR GEORGE WILL TAKE
NOTE OF THE NEW COURSE AND GET DOWN
TO THE NEXT SESSION. IT WOULD BE A SAD
LIFE WITHOUT GEORGE. ALSO WE RECOMEND IT
TO MIKE ACONLEY, WITH HIS VERY DODGY
LINESMAN POSITION.

VICTOR VICTORY

THIS EXCLUSIVE INTERVIEW WITH THE ONE AND ONLY VICTOR WELBURN TOOK PLACE BEFORE THE GAME WITH BROMPTON ON SATURDAY 9TH MARCH. MAURICE ACONLEY WAS ALSO PRESENT TO GIVE US HIS VALUABLE COMMENTS. IT IS REPRODUCED BELOW EXACTLY AS IT WAS SPOKEN WITH ABSOLUTELY NO CHANGES...

HORSE: What do you think of the fanzine?
VICTOR: It's brilliant!
HORSE: We think so aswell. What about the ground?
VICTOR: Which ground?
HORSE: Our ground! How does it rate with others in the league? Is it good?
VICTOR: Well, it's not too bad like. Bit exposed like. Could do with a stand for the fans...
HORSE: Yeh, with more and more fans now.
VICTOR: Yes.
HORSE: Do you think Barney would be able to cope with building a new stand?
VICTOR: Yees, aye, he's up to t'job is Barney.
HORSE: Yeh, he's a good lad is old Barney. Can you remember that reserve team match when we lost 28-0 to Westlers? Were you playing in it?
VICTOR: No I can't remember that!
MAURICE: What year was that?
HORSE: About 1986 or 5
VICTOR: Oh, I might do
HORSE: Yeh, I'm sure you were playing. We lost 28-0
VICTOR: Was it 28?
HORSE: Yeh, we can remember that!
VICTOR: Oh we only had 6 men though
HORSE: Did we?
VICTOR: 7 maybe
HORSE: Oh, I thought we had 11. Oh well. The reserve team were good weren't they?
VICTOR: Well, they were rubbish just before they broke up. But the first team pinched all their best players.
HORSE: They did. And do you think Mark Shepherd would be better if he didn't eat too many Mars bars?
MAURICE: Definitely!
VICTOR: Yes!
HORSE: And do you think he's fat?
VICTOR: Well built
HORSE: And what do you think of Andy Thrill and Brian Best?
VICTOR: Better off where they are, I think
HORSE: Yes. Right, this is all about national stuff. Who do you think is going to win the league?
VICTOR: Which league?
HORSE: The football league! The first division?
VICTOR: First division? Arsenal
HORSE: Who do you think is going to be the next Liverpool manager? Does Mick Barnes have a chance?
VICTOR: No chance!
HORSE: Which team do you support, except Thornton?
VICTOR: Secret!
HORSE: A secret?
VICTOR: Everton
HORSE: Everton? Oh, they're a good team are Everton, aren't they? Doing well this year! And what do you think of Scarborough and Man United, and Hull?

(CONTINUED ON NEXT PAGE)

VICTOR: Scarborough are not too bad like. Man United's over-rated
HORSE: And Hull? What about Hull aswell?
VICTOR: Hull? Oh, game for a laugh!
HORSE: Right what a marvellous interview, we'll put it in the next edition.
            We need a parting comment
VICTOR: Well, Brian, looks like Thornton need 3 points today, but I can't see
            'em gerrin' 'em
HORSE: Oh, what do you think of Eddie Avison's new hairstyle? Nice, isn't it?
VICTOR: Don't know. Don't know who his barber is, but I'm going to make sure
            I avoid him!

EXCLUSIVE! SHEEP SCANDAL

Well as you can see from the front cover our very own goalkeeper has been hiding
a very large secret from fellow players and supporters. The Escaped Horse were
casually flicking through the paper when they suddenly found themselves reading
an advertisement for blow up sex sheep! We had a little chuckle at this and were
just about to turn the page when we noticed that it was none other than the
Dales star keeper that was selling them! You can imagine the look on our faces,
we nearly died. Hurridly we rang up the main stockist and had a long conversation
about the sheep. As it turns out Stuart has been dealing sheep for about two years
now and as he works on a farm it is easy for him to hide his dubious trade.
We also learnt that the inflatable sheep were selling very well and according
to the records one of Stuarts main customers is none other than Andy Thrill the
ex Dale star! We have also heard from a nameless source that Mick Barnes and
Dean Richardson have something to do with these obscene goings on but as yet
we're not quite sure what. Is the entire Dale team turning quere, is Will
Balderson going to turn the corner cafe into a sheepwhore house, has Julian
Bevan moved to Snainton to open a sheep sex shop, is Victor Welburn and the
Escaped Horse Editorial team the only sane people left on the planet? hopefully
we'll be able to answer these obscure questions next issue.

We've said it before and we'll say it again 'don't believe everything you read
in the papers!'

PICKERING PERVERT

BRADLEY RUNS NAKED THROUGH STREETS OF PICKERING!!!
Well maybe thats a bit over the top but this story is absolutely true. A few
weeks ago Andy Thrill told us he had another exclusive for us and we thought
it was just going to be a crappy little story about Shep. How wrong we were.
Thrill revealed to The Escaped Horse an amazing true story about Richard
Bradley. According to Thrill, Bradley got very drunk one dark night in the
shady market town of Pickering, went up to the nearest unlucky female, got out
his rude part and told the poor girl to 'suck on this!' Of course the poor
lassie screamed and ran for the nearest policeman but this just shows that all
Dale players are actually raving, perverted lunatics. It just isn't safe to
walk the streets at night these days.
If we turn up to the next Dale game half dead blame Andy Thrill as he forced
us to print this story and Bradley threatened us not to!

IMPORTANT NOTICE TO ALL SUPPORTERS

Following a meeting of Dale supporters last month we are sorry to
inform you that we feel it may be time to call a halt to our rivalry
with Wykeham. Come on everyone, face the facts, they're absolutely
useless. How can we continue to have a rivalry with a club whose
abilities lie at the foot of the fourth division but are kept where
they are by a mixture of good luck and Brian Best?
It is a very difficult and unhappy dilemma for Dale but we must
consider an alternative rival more worthy of Dale's standing.
In view of these circumstances we feel that we must offer Wykeham

6 MONTHS NOTICE OF TERMINATION OF RIVALRY

At the end of this period if there is no sign of them being able to
offer Dale credible opposition then the rivalry will be at an end. In
the event of this happening the following action will be undertaken.
Thornton Dale will invite other clubs to:

TENDER FOR THE POSITION OF OUR NEW RIVALS

Applicants will be
At least as big as us
Within reasonable travelling distance of the yellow 'n' black army
With a history of things you've done to us
That we can get really pissed off about

****

Yes, we've got a really bad situation here, Wykeham are just too
flukey and crap that we feel it gives TDFC a bad name to be associated
with them. I mean, they are only in division 2 because of Besty's
goals and anyway, div 2 is utter shite, possibly worse than div 3, as
we showed by totally destroying Wykeham twice this season. In future
we need a team who can give us stiff competition, have done something
bad to us in the past, etc. Below are a few of our ideas for new
rivals......

LADY LUMLEYS SCHOOL UNDER 16's: These lot could match us and give us
a better game than Wykeham, they've defintely got a lot to answer for
because they are the culprits who presented us with Dean, Julian and
Lee!

WEETLERS UNITED RESERVES: Remember when these buggers beat us 29-0?
Yes, so do we. That was the game when we realised our reserve team was
utter dog turd and was later disbanded. We haven't forgiven them for
that...

THORNTON DALE DARBY AND JOAN CLUB X1: They're definitely more of a
football team than Wykeham, and on our current form could most
certainly give us a run for our money. They're situated close by so we
can pay them a visit once in a while...And they piss us off by taking
up all that room in the paper that should be reserved for us!

So there you have it, the perfect match! Lots of you will be thinking
we are stupid having rivals who don't even have a football team, but
the question must be asked, do we have a football team at the moment?

THORNTON DALE FC SUPPORTERS ARE PROUD TO ANNOUNCE OUR NEW RIVALS

THORNTON DALE DARBY AND JOAN CLUB

WYKEHAM REPORT

As the Dale didn't have a game last week and various other teams like Scarborough weren't playing, we all made the long trek to Snainton to see a potentially explosive 2nd division game between W***ham and West Pier. (There's no rest for us lot, you know). We also went to check out on Brian Best, he seems to score every week in the paper so we wanted to see this amazing occurence ourselves. Off we trundled and once we arrived we were met with a barrage of abuse from Besty, who shouted 'Scum.'' at us a number of times. It was even worse into the first half when Best opened the scoring with a completely flukey and utter shite goal that was miles offside anyway. He turned and ran towards us waving his arms about like a demented pigeon. Anyway, it was worth it in the end, the West Pier psycho's came back to lead 2-1 and their little mad indian midfielder Willy was calling Besty lots of nice names. West Pier had 2 men sent off, one for a beautiful elbow in the face right in front of us, and then Besty went on a crap run and swerved the ball between the post and the keeper for the equaliser. A really shite goal from a really shite player. Over all Wykeham were crap, even we could beat West Pier with 9 men. (Well, a slight exaggeration there) On the way back 5 of us had to cram into Mike's car but it was worth it all in the end because when we got home we realised that Leeds had lost!

ANIMAL   from the archives
number 1

Sensational news here from our famous fan and God-like figure Deggy Bond. On the way back from a crap Scarborough game, he was telling me about none other than Eddie Avison's dad in his playing days. If we thought Eddie was bad then you haven't heard anything yet. Deggy claims that Eddie's dad beat up absolutely anyone including the referee if they did anything wrong, and even if an opponent tackled him, it would be the signal for this 'animal' (quote Deggy Bond) to beat the shit out of him. And what's more, he was so bad that the league banned him for life! Shit, we'd hoped he would return some day to boost our midfield but obviously it's impossible now....

BRIDLINGTON FREE BOLLOCK

The report opposite was found in the pages of last week's Bridlington Free Press. Obviously they are completely bias towards the Mermaid scummers so we've rewritten the report below as we think it should be. Judge for yourself which is the most realistic.....

MERMAID are at the moment complete and utter flukey c**ts, kicking their way to the top of the crappest league in Britain. They have not lost for 7 games but that can't really be expected when playing shite teams like Ayton. Gooseneck, playing his first game since being beaten up by Deggy Bond two years ago, attacked the Ayton players and Green and Coe backed him up.
After the win against shite Ayton, Mermaid kick in Flamborough in their next fight, hopinh to show their strong and mental power. Goals were scored by Gooseneck with a flukey volley, Petch with a hard kick, Green and Bruno- Ward.

THE ESCAPED HORSE

WITH A FREE CRICKET FANZINE!

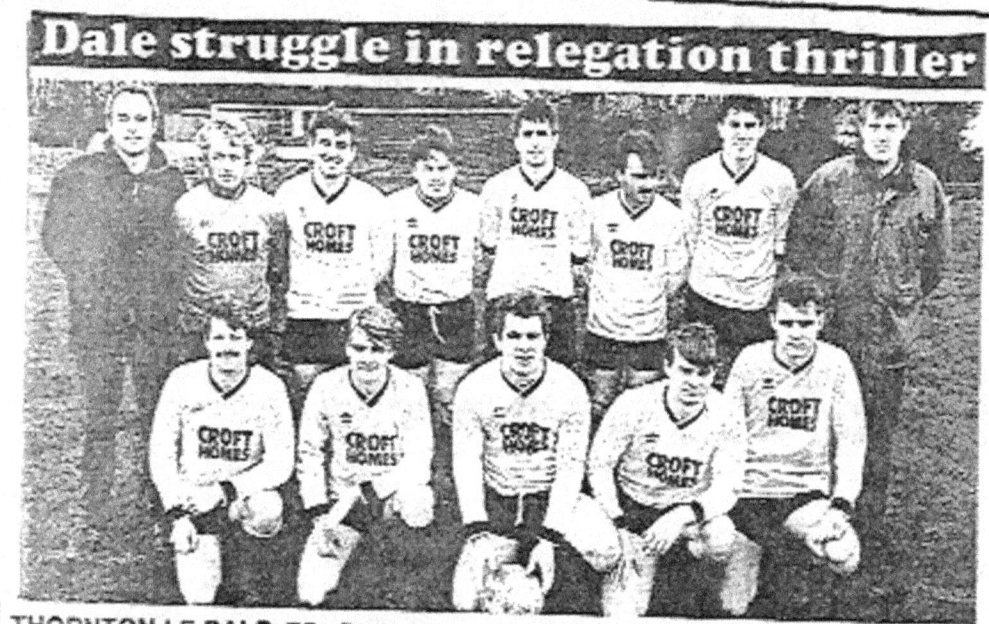

Dale struggle in relegation thriller

THORNTON-LE-DALE FC: Pictured from back left are M Aconley, S Hill, M Shepherd, A Johnson, W Balderson, S Dixon, J Bevan, M Barnes, R Smith, L Blackstone, G Baskeyfield, R Bradley and D Richardson

ANDY JOHNSON IN FACELIFT SENSATION!

SEE INSIDE

ALSO IN YOUR OUTSPOKEN AND OUTRAGEOUS HORSE : Ashley Welburn with another poem, We are famous, Great Whitby Sunday League Games of our time AND More!

GREYHOUND GRAPEVINE

EDITORIAL

Fame at last, as you'll see in the great pages to come, we've finally got into the paper! And a bloody lovely photo to go with it too, next thing you know we'll be on TV! Anyway this issue is the second last for this season (the last one will be done for the dinner) and as usual it's packed with great exclusives such as Andy Johnson's facelift, another amazing Ashley Welburn poem and a FREE cricket club fanzine! Yes it's true, the Escaped Martin Calvert. Sounds rather good eh?

THE AMAZING PHOTO'S THAT NEVER WERE

This issue would have had loads of marvellous photo's of Victor Welburn. Yes we trapesed all the way up to Lockton one Sunday morning to get a photo session with the almighty one and of course we got some great photo's of the God-like figure in action and they were to be published this issue, work the rest out for yourself...

QUOTES OF THE WEEK

PLAXTON PLAYER (The one with the tatoo on his leg) TO DEAN: "Run past me and I'll f**king shag yer!"
DEAN RICHARDSON (Just to get Leigh back): "Leigh and his eight ninths (Ask Sharon MOrley what this means)
YOUTH IN GARBUTS: "They're not doin' so well this season, Mick Barnes says it's because they get tired chasing after all the women!"

THANKS TO:
Martin Calvert, Ashley Welburn (Let's have another one!) Mike Aconley for playing again, The Gazette and Herald, Shaun Aconley for the photo's.
NO THANKS TO:
Team Plaxtons, Panasonic camera's, Mermaid FC, Andy Thrill for playing again....

****

FAT MAN ON THE RAMPAGE

Midfield magic? Ho Ho!

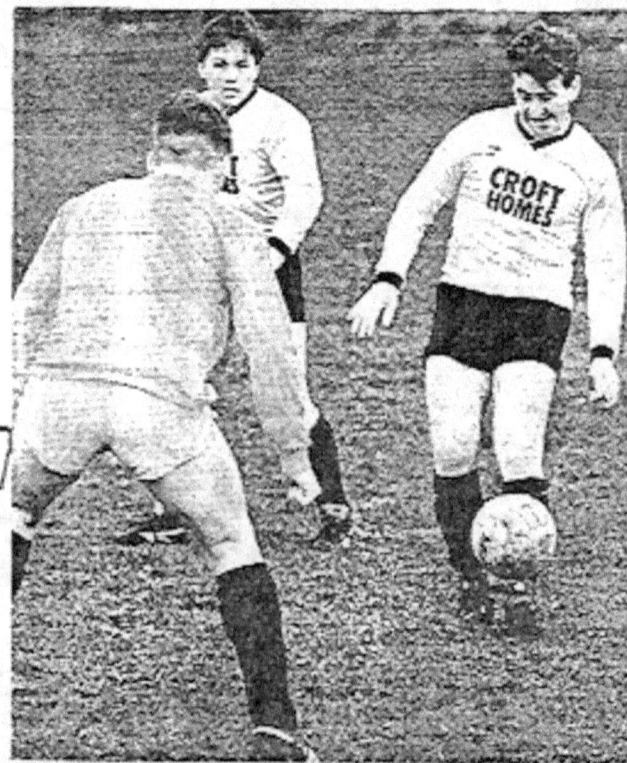

ON THE BALL: M Shepherd conjures up some midfield magic during Thornton-le-Dale's 6-4 home defeat in a Scarborough and District Third Division relegation battle

COVER STORIES

What's all this stuff about Andy Johnson then? Has he really had plastic surgery or is this story which we are about to tell you actually true?
Before the Filey game on Saturday Andy Rosher returned and obviously being our only slightly good player was shoved straight into the team. However, Mick Barnes and Mike Aconley realised everyone had to register before games to be able to play. Andy Johnson was registered but not at the ground, so Rosher was called Andy Johnson for the day. This all nearly backfired on the Dale management when the real Jono turned up half way through. Well within the referee's earshot, Barney remarked, 'Oh look, here's Andy Johnson!' The ref stared at Mick and the red faced joiner stuttered, 'Oh, I mean Andy Rosher!' Well we'll leave it to you to decide which of these stories is true....

****

PERVY PSYCHO

Well, we see Shaun Dixon has been up to his old tricks again. Obviously he can't resist team photographs! As you remember from issue 6 Dixon caused quite a stir with his antics with a certain Mr Thrill. The headline for that particular issue was 'Kinky Truth of Dale Stars', as if you don't remember!
Just look closely at the front cover, and follow Shaun Dixon's gaze to see where it ends up! Kinky beast! Also take note of Glen Baskeyfield fondling the ball! (PS- Will someone tell us why Dean always looks pissed?)

****

WIN SOME BOOZE

Yes, it's hard for a dead hard quiz this week, and we're deadly serious about it too. Use the answer sheet which you find provided and hand it to us before the end of season dinner, where the winner will be drawn. This lucky person will win two cans of lager from Costcutters, or orange juice if it's Julian because he's underage! Honestly, the winner WILL receive this prize, otherwise he can sue us!

1. Is this fanzine amazing?   A: Yes B: No C: Is Mike Scott God!
2. Can Dean take his ale?   A: Yes B: No C: He can't even take his lemonade!
3: What is Shaun Dixon?   A: A psycho B: Human C: A kinky Beast
4: How many times has Lee Brackstone told his dad to piss off during a game?
A: 0 B: 26 C: I'm deaf so how should I know!
5: Who is Andy Rosher? A: Andy Johnson B: A useless nobody C: Who?
6: What is Brian Best's famous saying: A: God, I'm shit! B: Oh, you're crap you lot!
C: I really miss playing football since I signed for Wykeham!
7: What is Mike Aconley's son called? A: Tarzan of the Apes B: Andy Thrill
C: Shaun
8: How many pints does Barney drink in one night? A: He's teetotal B: One or two
C: Enough to make him put Andy Thrill in the team last week?
9: What kind of car does Deggy Bond have: A: Psychadellic Beetle B: Lamborghini
C: A crappy yellow thing with no exhaust that smells of petrol!
10: What is Victor's favourite football side: A: Everton B: Wykeham C: Iraq

ASHLEY WELBURN WRITES AGAIN!

THE BATTLE OF MERMAID

It was on that fateful Saturday
When Mermaid came up here to play
We'd heard they could play well enough
But we'd also heard they could cut up rough!

We needed a strong ref to keep the job right
But as we entered the ground we were met with the sight
Of George with his dogs and his battered old van
"I'll keep this lot straight lads, I'm sure I can!"

George had his book out in the very first minute
He wouldn't be happy till he had a few in it!
"You'll have to go off! I told you before!"
As the battle developed into a war

"What did you do that for?
That's a home free kick there!"
His falsetto expressions were piercing the air
Then he did something further to hurt Mermaid's pride
By allowing Dale a goal that was a mile offside!

Bradders was singled out for some abuse
Their full back was like a bull turned loose
It was tough on young Rich – he was only a lad
And it didn't go down well with Rich's dad

Hurtling from nowhere came Carl the yob
To smack captain Derek right in the gob!
As Derek turned round to look for the thug
He hit the small youth in the lug!

"This ref is a dickhead!" A Mermaid cried
"Let's all leave the pitch now, the whole bloody side!"
And that was what happened, they were led off the pitch
By a youth who appeared to have crawled from a ditch

George stood on the touch line, his foot on the ball
Would there be any more play, at all?
Dale sat on the pitch – they behaved very well
Mermaid stayed off it, moaning like hell!

The Gooseneck with long hair and a gap in his teeth
Seemed their worst offender for causing the grief
"I wish you'd stop moaning, you ugly get!"
Said Shep as he hid behind the net!

"We can't stop here all day," said the referee
"If we dawdle much longer I'll miss me tea!"
They decided to re-start. Back into the breach!
Hacking and kicking at ow't they could reach

The end of the match – back to get changed
And still the Mermaids were acting deranged
A Gobbit of spittle shot fair and square
Ended up in a Thornton Dale player's hair

CONTINUED ON NEXT PAGE

THE BATTLE OF MERMAID   CONTINUED

Deggy had stirred it as much as he could
He wouldn't be happy until he's seen blood
His wish was granted as on leaving the pitch
A Mermaid yob planted him one on the snitch!

It was so long ago can't remember the score
But I know that we won and we got four
What a fiasco! That's all you can say
The day Mermaid came to the Dale to play

PS: Please keep this away from Mermaid or I'm a dead man!

TAW

****
EDITORIAL NOTE: Wow, sensational, unbelievable. We at TEH don't know why Ashley
didn't decide to be a professional poet. We couldn't believe anyone could write
poems so well! This is of course the second masterpiece handed in through
the sacred letterbox, and it gets better each time! So a free edition to Ash and
we are suffering withdrawal symptoms — send us another one quick!
****

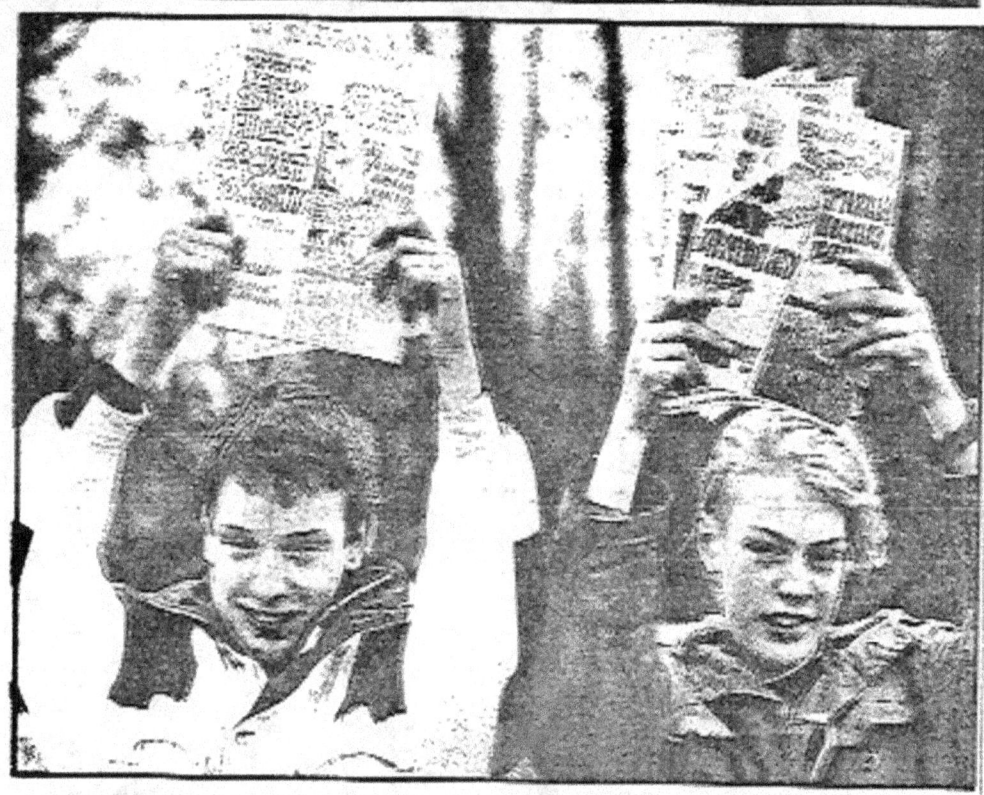

Soccer players laugh at The Escaped Horse

THE Escaped Horse leaves Thornton-le-Dale football players and supporters curled up with laughter after the hard slog on the field every Saturday.

Three Thornton-le-Dale teenagers, who all go to Lady Lumley's School in Pickering, write an alternative-style match magazine called The Escaped Horse, which they sell at home games.

The publication, with a weekly circulation of 25, is bursting with satirical articles and slapstick tales of football exploits.

The talented editorial team includes 14-year-old Steven Allardice, of Church Lane, Thornton-le-Dale, and the Stanniforth brothers from the High Street, Paul, aged 14, and Mark, aged 16.

The senior member of the comedy trio, Mark, explained that the main aim of the magazine is to make fun of the players.

"It's mostly mickey taking and it gives the players a bit of a laugh. They read it in the pub after the game and they laugh if it's about someone else.

"They're not too bothered if it's about them, but they all look forward to the next issue."

The embarrassing exposes on Thornton-le-Dale players would be hard for the best investigative reporters to uncover but Mark told the Gazette & Herald his secret.

He just interviews the players to get them to spill the beans on each other and The Escaped Horse is never short of material with fresh editions for almost every home game.

The strange name of the football magazine was chosen after a horse escaped from the soccer field during a match. The game was stopped while the players tried to catch the horse.

WINNING TEAM: Paul Stanniforth and Steve Allardice hold the front page

Fame at last, eh? The Horse is now officially recognised by the Gazette, even
though one or two things are written wrongly like 'It's mostly mickey taking'.
We could have sworn that we said 'It's mostly taking the piss' when they
rang up to interview us. Oh well, that's life....

FROM THE ARCHIVES

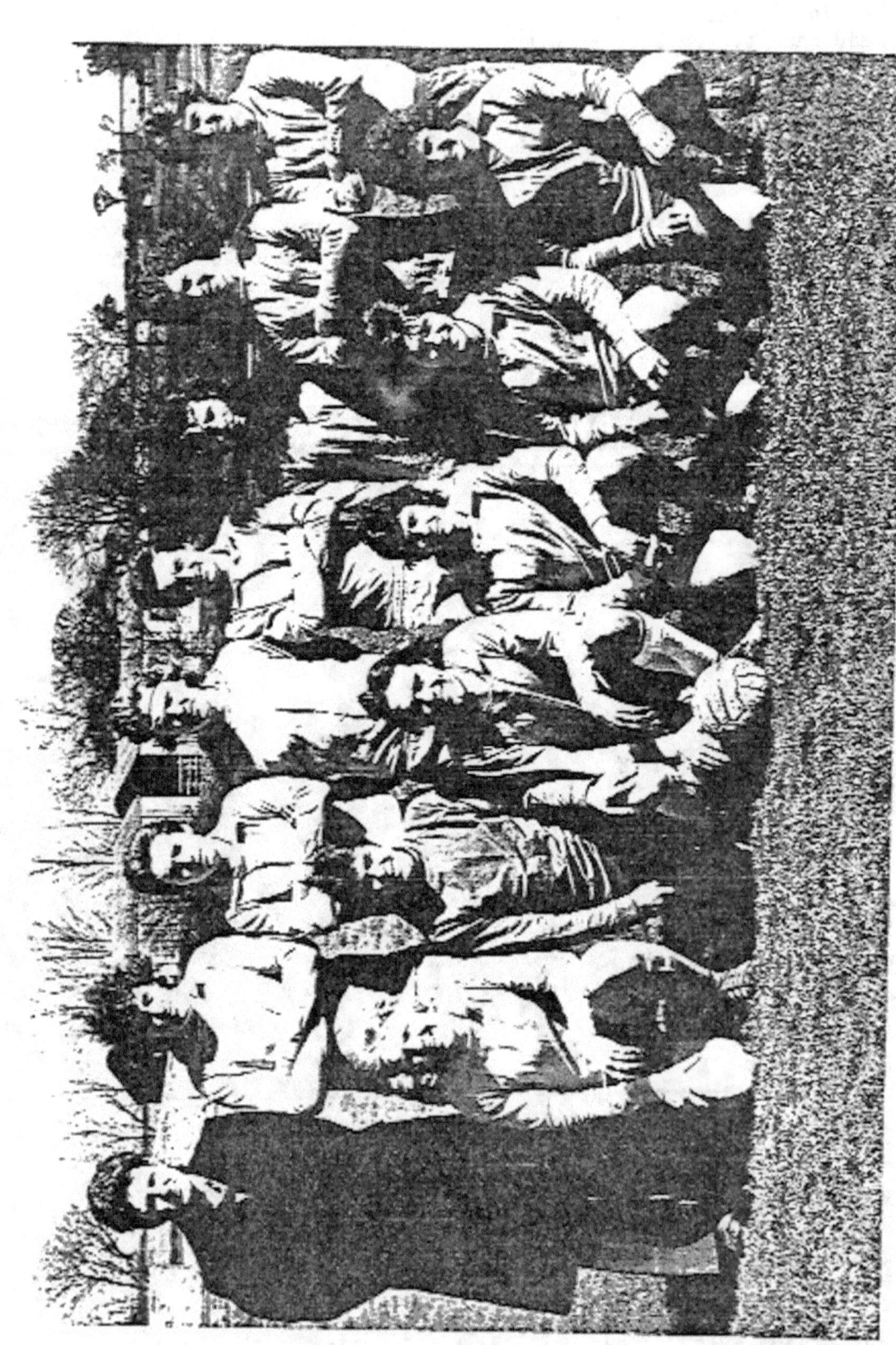

JUST LOOK AT MIKE AND BARNEY'S HAIRCUTS!
(PS - IS THAT MR BRACKSTONE IN THE TOP LEFT?!?)

FREEZING WITH THE FISHERMEN

ANOTHER REMARKABLE GROUNDHOPPING EXPERIENCE

Everybody must think that Dale are the worst team on the planet at the moment. However, your EH editorial team, always the optimists, are desperate to prove you wrong. We have decided to go to any lengths to find a worse team than Thornton Dale. We realised it would take some doing and great expense with bus fares to far flung corners of North Yorkshire. But we decided to do it just for you, to give you some encouragement next time you wear that famous yellow and black. And the next time you wear a Thornton shirt aswell.

It had to be somewhere obscure, so after reading all the local papers in Bradleys sorry, Garbuts, I decided to plump for the Whitby Sunday league and the delights of Fishermen v Star Inn, after seeing the advert below in the 'Whitby Gazette'. Of course it meant forward planning so immediately after watching Scarborough fluke their usual three points at home I went up to Whitby for the night. It cost £2 for the bus fare, but I perked up when I remembered I was doing it especcially for Dale and that they would appreciate my efforts, ho ho.

And there I was, Sunday April 14th, The Showground, Whitby, miles from anywhere, a hurricane raging, and freezing my bollocks off. It was 10.15 in the morning and I was knackered. Then I saw a lovely fat man in a red coat strolling across the 'pitch' during the warm up. 'Who's playing?' I asked. 'CRAP GIT!' he yelled back and I wondered what I had said. I soon realised he had been talking to the goalkeeper who had just missed an easy shot. When he calmed down he told me. 'Fishermen's in blue, an' Star's in green an' white 'oops'. The whistle blew and I stood, watching two lumps of shite kicking a piece of leather about.

A Star player made a mess of a clearance and was told by an observer that 'You're still f***ing pissed, Wayne!' Such friendly folk, these Whitby lot. I still had to hear a swearword free sentence. The wind was still raging and it was bloody freezing. Of course I was spurred on by the thought that all Sunday League games seem to have immensely high scores, 10-1, 8-3, 6-4 etc. Trust me to choose one where no goals were scored after 40 minutes. Meanwhile on the pitch opposite there were goals galore. (Well, two anyway). Then I couldn't believe it. Star scored. It was so good I don't remember anything about it. Half time. Icicles were now forming on the cross bar, and I was staring at my watch, hoping the pitch would be unplayable for the second half so that I could go home.

Five minutes into the second half a Fisherman crossed the ball and it was flicked in for the equaliser. Then all hopes of a good second half were dashed. It was utter shite for the remaining 35 minutes. As soon as the whistle went I ran away trying to keep warm and brushing the ice off my coat. It was good. Well, it's always good when it's finished, isn't it? You can hold your head up high and boast, 'I went to a Whitby Sunday League game last week, and I lasted the full 90 minutes'. Wow.

But the real reason I went was to find a team worse than Thornton. I hoped one would be, otherwise I'd have to go to another far-flung hole sometime. Were they worse than Thornton? Were they bollocks. Anyone for Ganton?

Star Inn (v Fishermens, Sunday at Showfield meet 9.45am ko 10.15am; v Danby and Castleton, Tuesday at Showfield meet 5.45pm ko 6pm; v Fylingdales Thursday at Fylingthorpe meet Station Square 5.45pm, Helredale 5.55pm ko 6pm).

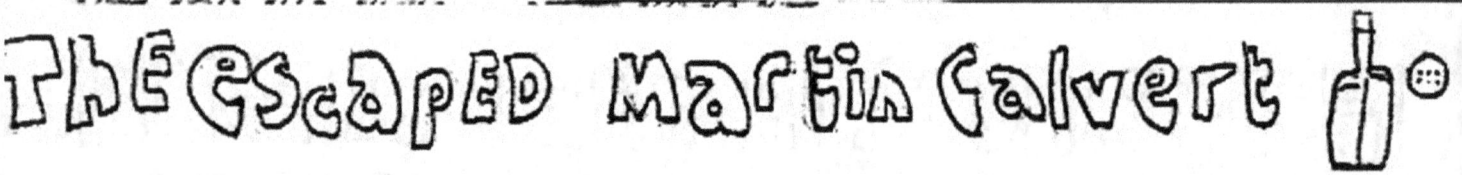

THE ESCAPED MARTIN CALVERT

A FREE THORNTON DALE CRICKET CLUB FANZINE. 1st & ONLY ISSUE

GIVEN AWAY FREE WITH YOUR ESCAPED HORSE

IT'LL BE HERE SOON! by Martin Calvert

Yes, we're nearly there folks! It's nearly that time of year again when we can
put our boxes down our trousers and settle down to lovely 3 day cricket
matches in the beautiful summer weather. If you fancy donning the Dale
flannels, see Martin Calvert for more details. Alternatively if you want a bit
of pre-season practise see the noticeboard or ring Martin Calvert for more details.
The fixtures have been made and our first meeting is at the picturesque Forge
Valley. Martin Calvert will be arranging travel for those who need it.
****
AWAY FROM THE STUMPS by Martin Calvert

Beginning with raffle news and the winner of the recent Cricket Club raffle,
drawn by Martin Calvert, was Martin Calvert himself. The raffle raised valuable
funds for the club, which were gladly accepted recently by the treasurer,
Martin Calvert. Another success was the Grand National sweepstake, organised
and drawn by Martin Calvert. The winner with Seagram was none other than Martin
Calvert and once again all proceeds were donated on behalf of the club to the
treasurer Martin Calvert. Everyone has appreciated his fine work and at the
recent AGM secretary Martin Calvert proposed a vote of thanks. They also voted in
new offficials at the AGM, and these are as follows: PRESIDENT: Martin Calvert
CHAIRMAN: Martin Calvert. SECRTARY: Martin Calvert. TREASURER: Martin Calvert.
Winner of the Martin Calvert trophy for best player in Martin Calvert's opinion
during last season was Martin Calvert.
****
GROUND NEWS by Martin Calvert

The ground is a bit bumpy at the present, so Martin Calvert will be spear-heading
a task force of volunteers to push the roller and even the pitch out. For more
details ring Martin Calvert or turn up at the ground on Sunday at 9.00am and
find Martin Calvert immediately. New seats have been installed in the pavilion
by Martin Calvert, paid for out of club funds by Martin Calver. The treasurer
Martin Calvert made the money available. If you would like to see Martin Calvert
test them out, come down on Sunday. Again more details can be obtained from
Martin Calvert.
****
GENERAL NEWS by Martin Calvert

Martin Calvert will be running the London marathon to raise funds for the club,
all sponsorships would be appreciated by treasurer Martin Calvert, or just Martin
Calvert himself. As we said earlier more players are urgently wanted and Martin
Calvert will be delighted to speak to any intersted parties. Ring Martin
Calvert yet again for yet more details.
****
FUNNY HAPPENINGS by Martin Calvert

Shaun Aconley will be raising money for the club during the first game of the season,
after a discussion with Martin Calvert. Martin Calvert suggested that Shaun should
balance on the fence and climb trees during the entire match. Martin Calvert is
delighted that youngsters should be interested in the club, a view echoed by
secretary Martin Calvert. Treasurer Martin Calvert was unavailable for comment.
****
CHARITY NEWS by Martin Calvert

During last year's Pickering Carnival, mars bars were thrown into the crowds from the
float by Mark Shepherd.

THE ESCAPED HORSE

ISSUE 14

EXCLUSIVE

EXCLUSIVE

MARK SHEPHERD ADMITS IN CRICKET MATCH SENSATION:

I AM FAT

FULL STORY INSIDE!

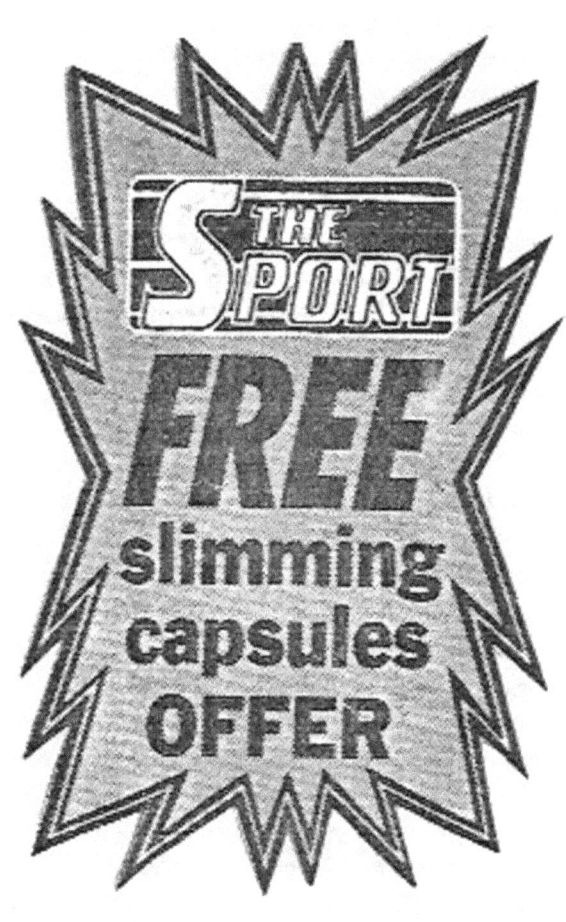

THE SPORT FREE slimming capsules OFFER

FREE!

CHIP FORK TO EAT YER DINNER WITH!

GREYHOUND GRAPEVINE

EDITORIAL.

Well here we are at the end of such a thrilling season. We'd really just like to say thanks to everyone who has contributed and bought the fanzine this season. Ta. See you at Ganton.

WELBURN STARTS OFF NEW CRAZE.

Yes it's the return of the 1970's as anyone at the Ryedale game will have realized. Victor has returned and with him he brings the new craze, 1970's red headbands!! Hopefully next season we'll be selling red headbands along with your copy of The Escaped Horse. By the way Victor was the only one who played any good last week so get a red headband and you might be as good as Vic! take note Dean.

AMAZING FREE GIFTS

Well we hope you enjoy your pie and chips tonight and just to make life a bit easier for you we've given you a FREE chip fork to eat your dinner with. Saves using them fingers doesn't it?

THE LONG LOST POEM

No we still haven't got it, what is Andy Johnson playing at? For Gods sake give us the bloody poem. What are you afraid of? If it slags us off we won't print it and if it slags you off we'll print it in every edition. Just send us the bloody thing!

THE BESTY POEM

We're terribly sorry about what is written below but it had to come sooner or later.

WE SLAGGED HIM OFF
ALL SEASON LONG
AND NOW TO WYKEHAM
HE HAS GONE

WE'VE TRIED TO DISGUISE IT
THE BEST WE COULD
BUT WE HAVE TO ADMIT
BRIAN BEST IS GOOD

THANKS TO

Brian Best	Andy Thrill	Victor Welburn	Ashley Welburn
Mick Barnes	Mike Aconley	Thornton Chippie	Goodmans Chippie
Moorlands	Garbutts	Darren Acombs Printer	The Gazette
The Brompton keeper	The Scarbro fanzine	The QPR fanzine	
Deggy Bond	and most of all everyone whose bought this rag		

COVER STORY EXCLUSIVE

It had to happen sooner or later, didn't it? After all that pressure we've been putting on young Mark Shepherd, he finally cracked at the recent cricket match against Rievaulx. One of your intrepid editors made some comment about mars bars and young Mr Shepherd turned round. Was he going to hit us? Spit on us? Tell us to f**k off? No, incredibly he uttered the following: "I KNOW I'M FAT, BUT STOP TAKING THE PISS, I CAN'T HELP IT!" We nearly fainted with shock. Was he pissed? No, Mark Shepherd was finally confessing. Full marks to the lad for plucking up the courage to admit it straight to us. We admire him so much that for the next two lines we will not slag him off at all.

Well there it was, the young man reckoned that he couldn't help it, so we have come up with the following five points to rid him of this weight problem...

1. Stop eating mars bars
2. Stop eating Snickers bars
3. Stop eating Twix bars
4. Stop eating Bounty bars
5. Stop eating Milky Ways

Next season we promise to donate £1 to club funds for every stone Shep loses in weight. With a bit of luck the club could make a couple of hundred quid!

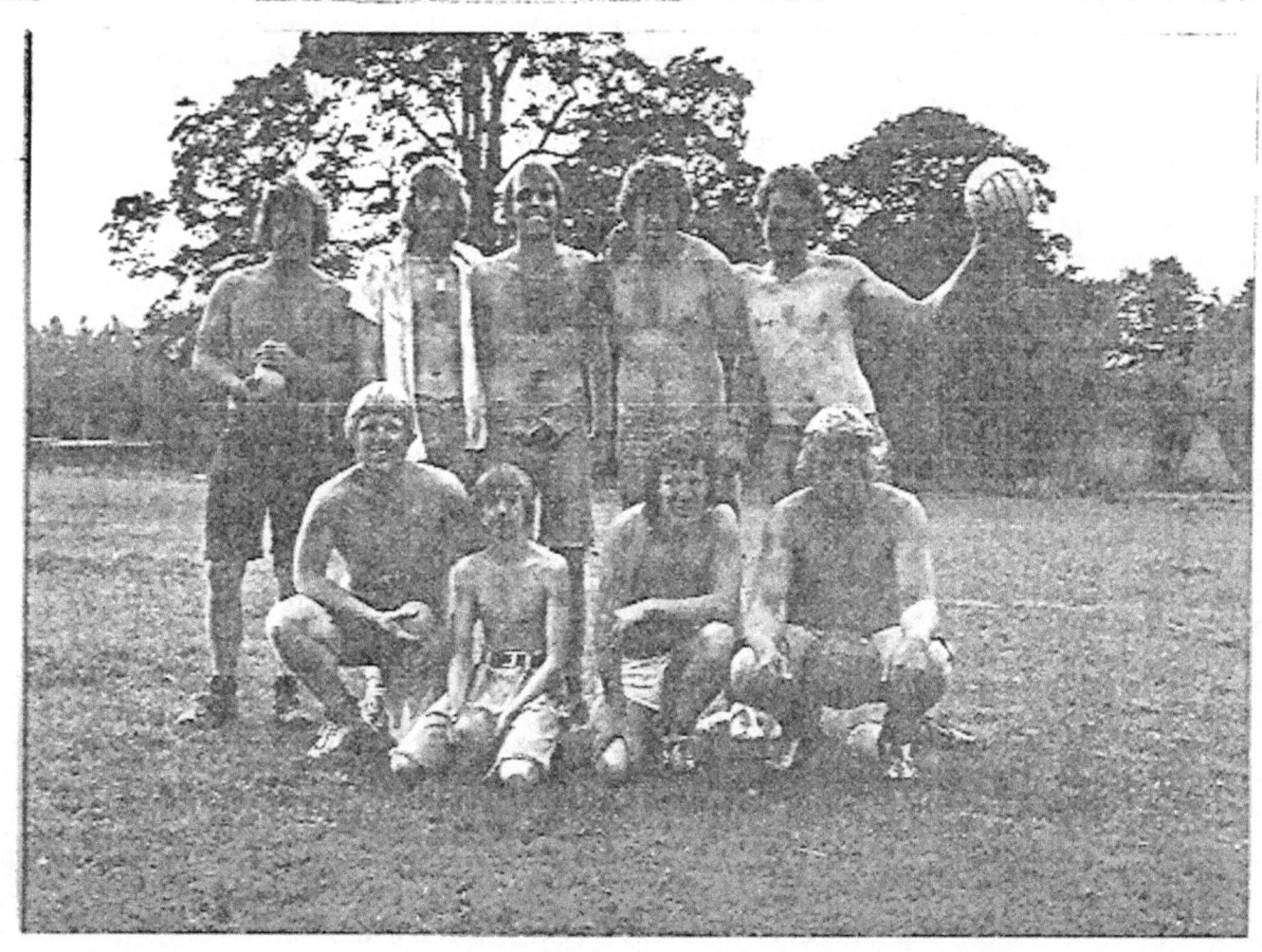

There's no point making a witty comment, we think it speaks for itself...

REVIEW OF THE E.S OVER THE SEASON

It all started in August last year. After having a slight idea for quite a long time about starting up a fanzine, we decided it was time to act and to produce at least one issue. The first problem was the title. We thought about something to do with greyhounds, such as 'Greyhound Gazette', but a firm favourite was 'And I suppose you think that's funny?' commemorating the words of a referee after members of the editorial team had continuously questioned his parentage throughout the first half. Even 'Victor' was discussed but there was already a comic with that name so it was discounted. Then, suddenly, one of the editors' had a brainwave. If you don't know why we called it this, where have you been for the last 2 months? 'THE ESCAPED HORSE' was born.

Looking back at issue 1 now, we have to admit it was crap. However, when we had just done it, we thought it was a masterpiece. We even put on the top of the one page mag, 'Not bad for only 15p'. All it consisted of was a few phrases and a feature entitled 'Why is Andy Hill called Snebber?'. Issue 2 hit the streets with a massive four pages. However, one of these was blank with the others made up of the usual 'grapevine' type articles such as 'Brian Best - the facts', one page of match reports, and another which slagged off Ganton and Mermaid and included the first ever Escaped Horse poem.

The sensationalism began to creep in by issue 3 as we carried a feature 'Bevan - the truth'. Again match reports and more exclusive stories such as 'Snebber returns' and 'Leeds fan gets in at Luton'. This issue was entirely word-processed on a friend's computer, however it buggered up the printer after doing 20 copies, so we were forced into typing out issue 4. Typing though costs money and God repaired the WP in time for issue 4 and after much reluctance from the owner we were allowed to use it again! The cover carried a 'Sensational World Exclusive' with Brian Best's first ever letter to the editors. This was written just before the game with Wykeham and a lovely quote was 'Sorry you'll be making an early Cup exit'. The Word Processor really went wrong this time so we splashed out on a tape to typewrite number 5.

We just had to remind Besty of the score the previous Saturday so in our own delicate way the cover of issue 5 consisted of two fingers and the headline, 'Sod off Besty!' We proudly proclaimed this to be the 'We Bashed Besty' edition. Inside there were match reports, articles on the grapevine included 'Andy Hill is going bald' and there were also league tables and a tribute to George Revely - the greatest referee ever.

However, it was issue 6 which changed the whole future of the fanzine. This was the first in a long line of sexual exclusives with the famous photo of Shaun Dixon giving Andy Hill a good going over and the headline, 'Kinky truth of Dale stars' We also found a raunchy tale about our proposed tour of Holland and a world exclusive photo of Mick Barnes appeared inside. There was also an amazing interview with Mick's son Craig, who sensationally informed us that 'Shep eats too many cherries!' Whatever you say Craig. To cut down on photocopying costs Steven decided to get issue 7 done at Burgess'. The usual format was buggered and one page even turned out pink! The headline was 'Dale crisis' and our serious article inside prompted much criticism from the officials. In future we'd stick to their sizzling secrets. There is a photo of Dean, a profile of Julian and we even predicted at that early stage that we would go down! Gypsies or what?

CONTINUED ON NEXT PAGE

Issue 8 was the amazing 8 page christmas edition. Two page of stars, a sensational ground photo and "Confessions of a Brompton "keeper" were included and this would be the first issue to carry a player of the year update - according to this Shaun Dixon, Will Balderson seem the main bets for the cup.

Number 9 was also revolutionary - it was photocopied the wrong way round. The front cover carried the headline "The Back Cover" and the major story consisted of "Thrill's injury fraud" and "Star man Bradley left in shop!" There was another Besty letter and photo, an exclusive pic of Glen, and Dean revealed that striker Shaun Dixon was a psycho. Issue 10 saw the title "Eddie in Bush Bash" and saw the first sensational Ashley Welburn poem. This was the only edition to carry a story about Mark Shepherd that was so bad it had to be censorded! At the last moment we thought it was so bad that it just could not be included - however with a bit of persuasion and the slipping of a few quid we could put it in the next issue! There was an action photo and a picture of a team called "Wankers FC". Wonder who they could be...

On now to number 11 which saw two exclusive photo's from Dale's rich heritage. There were features entitled "Andy shares his thrills", "Beer glass saga" and "Barnes for Liverpool?" alongside "Dale's subbuteo team" and the now sadly departed "Back to the future" page. There was also an offer for "Andy Hill red conks". Then came the Brompton game, this opportunity was too good to miss so a free 1 page special was brought out. The Brompton issue was basically slagging off the manager!

Issue 12 was a massive exclusive issue where Stuart Hills secret company was exposed. This issue really was something as it also contained the Randy Thrill interview and more of besty's brilliant/pathetic letters.

Andy Johnson in facelift sensation was the front cover sporting a lovely photo of our shit team.
This was also the time when we came famous and appeared in the always right Gazette. Also in this issue Ashley Welburn showed more class talent with a poem about none other than M*****d.

****

Thornton-le-Dale grab title

IS THERE SOMETHING WE SHOULD KNOW ABOUT?

PLAYER OF THE YEAR

Well, it's dinner time again folks, which means it's the time of year again to give out our praises or otherwise to the players who've turned out for the Yellows over the past few months. Here goes with an individual review of each star:

ANDY THRILL: Only played a few games and even hit the net a few times in the early stages. Could have been a contender for 'Player of the Year' award but half the time he was off playing cricket and shagging those Ozzie lassies!

ANDY JOHNSON: Faked an injury to get out of playing but he's been a good supporter. Otherwise there's nothing to say about him because he's such a boring git!

MICK BARNES: Brick shithouse in defence when he's played, and part time Scalby striker. What a lovely header, Michael!

MIKE ACONLEY: The Gazette are obviously in love with him but only played when we were desperate and we could see why!

VICTOR WELBURN: This God-like figure played like Pele in the second half of our last game and on the strength of that performance alone he almost snatched the player of the year award. Obviously that red headband does something for him!

STUART HILL: Great performer all through the season, a leading contender for the award, those thrills he got from the sheep obviously helped!

MARK SHEPHERD: This anorexic-looking defender has been consistent throughout the season but with a few less mars bars he could have done a bit better.

NICK VERMONT: Who?

WILL BALDERSON: Psycho defender/midfielder who'll stop at nothing to get the team motivated. A good consistent performer who was even trying when we were 6-0 down against Ryedale!

MARK BAGNELL: This Feargal Sharkey lookalike was ok at right back but gradually faded away so much that we often mistook him for a blade of grass.

SHAUN DIXON: Probably top- scorer and one of our better players which isn't really saying much. Good at throw ins and shots from the half way line.

JULIAN BEVAN: This young tiger has played out of his schoolboy skin throughout the season but his loyalty must be questioned after missing the odd game because he got pissed on the night before. Well done for coming to Filey, though.

RAYMOND SMITH: For a veteran he was suprisingly good in defence and kept plugging away throughout the 1990/1 season.

LEE BRACKSTONE: This young midfielder has shown the occasional flash of brilliance and his silky skills were where the chant 'Skin 'im' originated. Amusing when he begins to argue with daddy, too.

GLEN BASKEYFIELD: Probably top scorer too, (well how the f**k do we know?) best for his celebrating of his goals and another consistent performer.

RICHARD BRADLEY: Steven says he was completely shite all season and although we take no responsibility for Steven's views, we agree with him this time!

DEAN RICHARDSON: Young Deany Rick is our 'super-sub' - thank God he stays as a 'super-sub' and never gets on to the pitch!   .

****

So if you're reading this before the presentation, you know who the contenders are, obvious favourite being the one and only Deany Rick. Nick Vermont is another leading name, but you'll just have to wait and see won't you, you impatient b***ards!

WE AGAIN THINK THESE SPEAK FOR THEMSELVES, NICE HAIRCUT BARNEY!

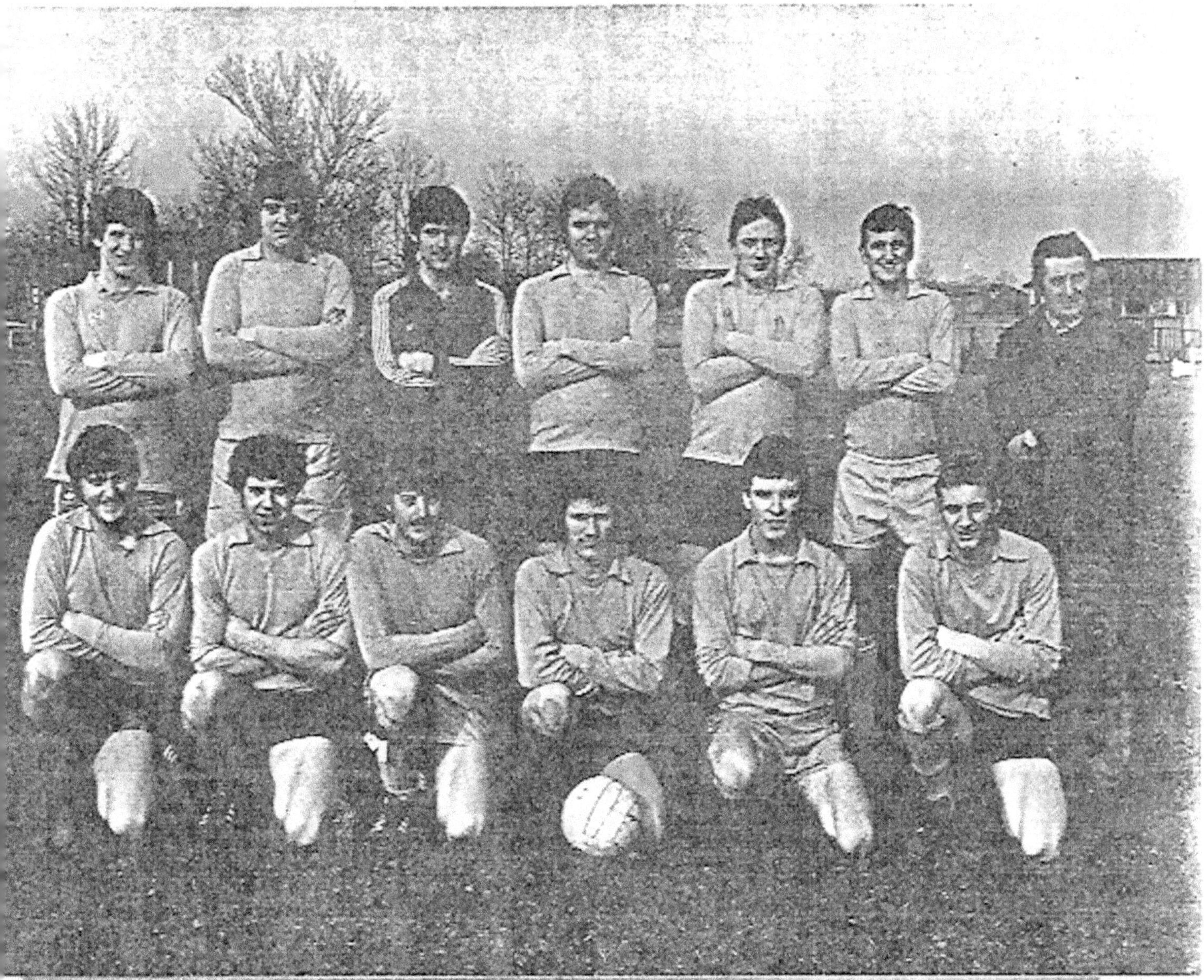

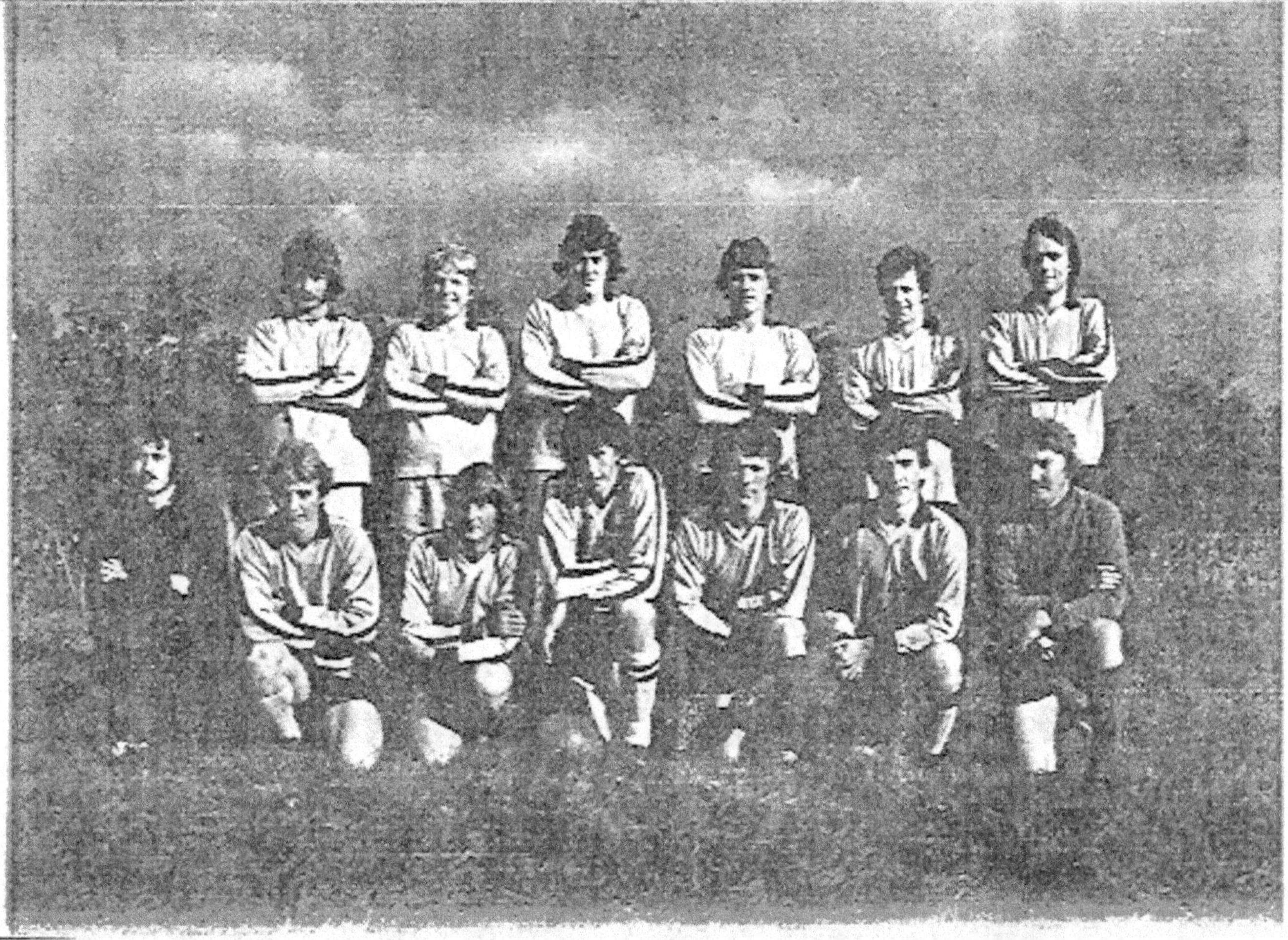

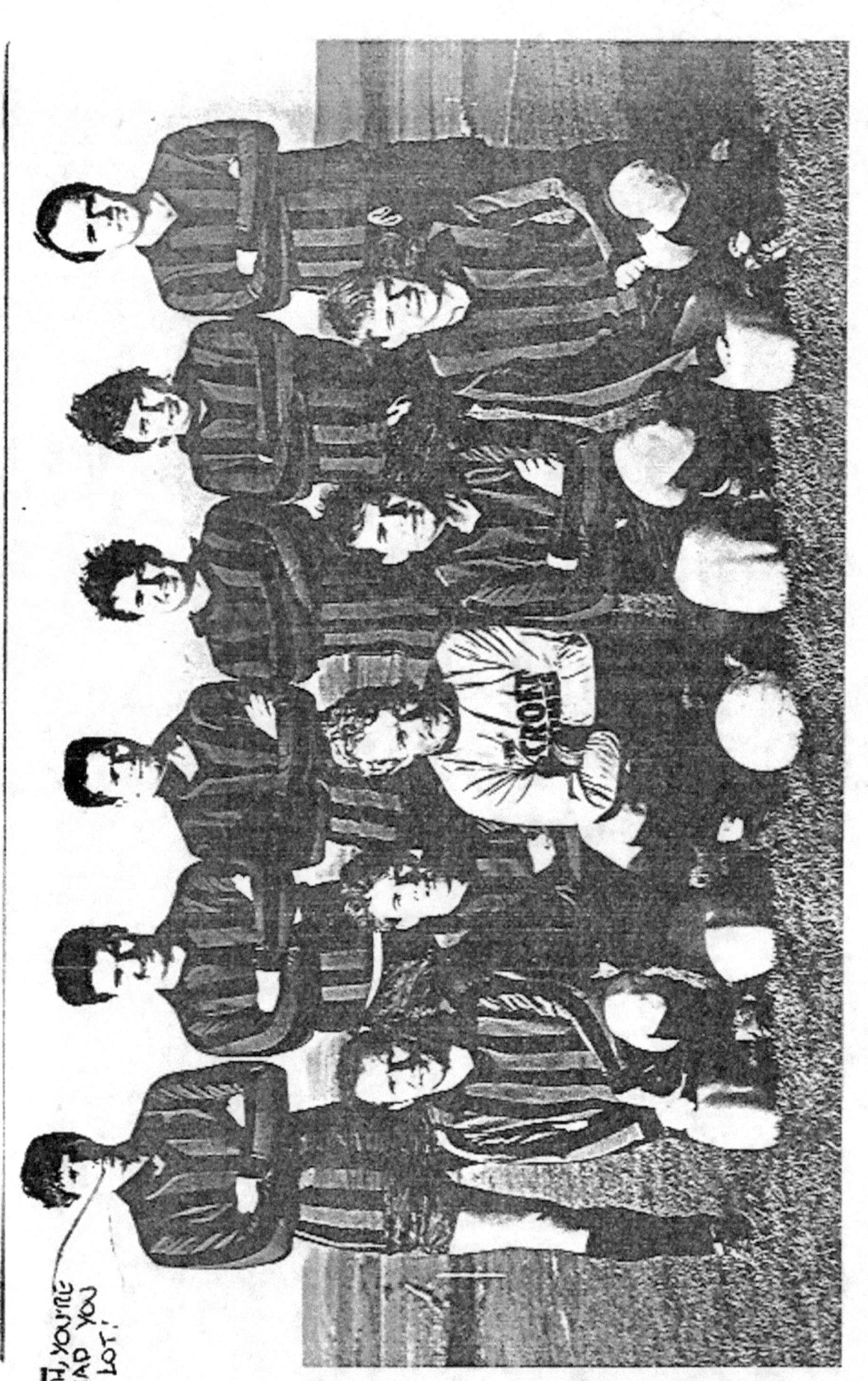

'OH, YOU'RE CRAP YOU LOT!'

BACK ROW: LEFT TO RIGHT (B.GG'S BACK TO FRONT/ROW) BEST, ?, ?, VINNY JONES, FATBOY, VIC REEVES, 'THE ONE AND ONLY'

FRONT ROW: E. (STARS A WIG!) ANISON, TOP GOALSCORER (WITH 2!) REFEREMENT LOOMS, MR THRILL, GROUNDSMAN

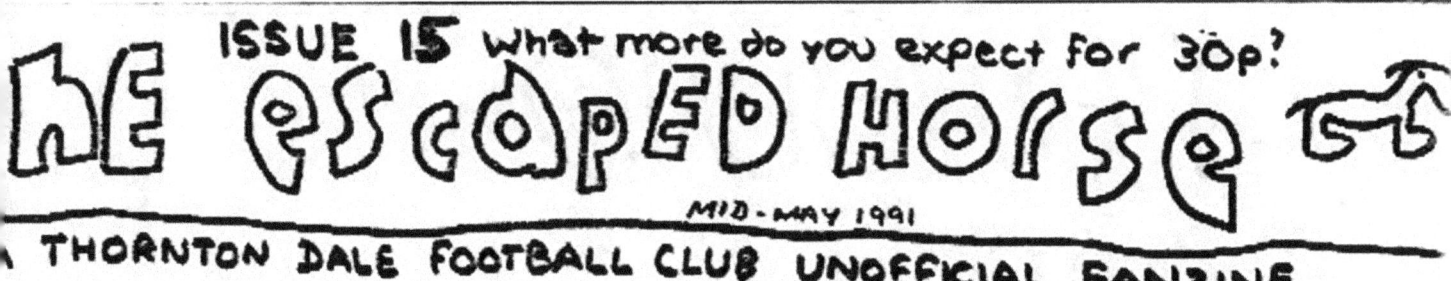

ISSUE 15 what more do you expect for 30p?

HE ESCAPED HORSE

MID-MAY 1991

THORNTON DALE FOOTBALL CLUB UNOFFICIAL FANZINE

INSIDE THESE 8 PAGES BURSTING WITH LITERARY DELIGHT:

RALPH SPEAKS OUT!

STUNNING REVELATIONS TO SHOCK THE WORLD

YET ANOTHER WORLD EXCLUSIVE FROM THE ESCAPED HORSE

PLUS: SENSATIONAL DINNER REPORT FROM 1906!

he *Catechism* naturally divides itself into fit
ions.

1. Exposition of the Baptismal Covenant.
2. The Creed and its explanation.
3. The Ten Commandments and their explanation.
4. The Lord's Prayer and its explanation.
5. The doctrine of the Sacraments.

1. *Exposition of the Baptismal Covenant.*

he reader must bear in mind that the whol

PARISH MAGAZI

Vol. XIX.—No. 4.　　APRIL, 1906.　　Price

GREYHOUND GRAPEVINE

EDITORIAL

Through popular demand, we're back already in these desert conditions called the British summer. Although this is not the football season any more, we're getting enough stuff to probably bring out one or two more before September. So keep buying it and send something to us. If you're pissed off at having to splash out another 30p, blame Andy Thrill - he wanted another issue out!

****

NEXT SEASON

We are hoping next year to bring out a new edition for every home game, so that we can slag off our opponents and do not have to sell 25 issues at places like Filey where only 8 people bother to turn up. As far as we know it'll still be 8 pages for 30p, unless the Scarborough FA live up to their usual standards and give us 7 home games in 1 week, in which case they'll only be 1 page issues for some games.
****

RESERVE RETURN CAMPAIGN

Yes that's right, we're launching a campaign to get our reserves back. They gave us some wonderful memories, such as the 28-0 home defeat v Westlers (see next issue) and the 6-0 win over Kirkbymoorside reserves when the keeper was very friendly towards us ('Shut your f**king gobs and f**k off!') There obviously is a shortage of players, but what about Ralph, Ashley, Steve Avison, Richard Thorner, Besty, etc? More details and the launching of the campaign in the next issue...
****

GREAT INTERVIEW OF ALL TIME?

Thanks to Ralphie for the sensational interview, we're hoping to make these a regular occurence from now on, so watch out!
****

IS EDDIE PREGNANT?

We don't have a clue what it's about, but Richard Bradley keeps pleading with us to say 'when's it due' to Eddie. So we have. More info please, what's this about?
****

THANKS TO: The Cardiff fanzine 'Intifada', Ralph, TDFC reserves for the memories.
NO THANKS TO: Mermaid (well what else do we write here?) Andy Thrill for going on holiday so we can't get any exclusives on him this week.

QUOTES OF THE SUMMER:
VICTOR (entering the Buck on the dinner night): 'Is this where t'shindig is?'
SHEP: 'I am fat'

NEXT ISSUE: Exclusive interview with Andy Thrill's knackered radio(!), reserve campaign launched, and is Thrill really off to Ozzie?

****

RALPH INGLEBY SPEAKS OUT

If there was a prize for the most controversial, unbelievable, hilarious interview ever to have taken place, the following would have won easily. We're getting used to giving you exclusives, but this really is the big one. The answers below are written EXACTLY as Ralph said them (if you don't believe us ask Shep - he was there). To get full enjoyment from the following, imagine the answers being spoken in Ralphie's own sacred voice... Here goes...

NAME:	You know my name you daft cunt!
BIRTHDATE:	What's up now?
PREVIOUS CLUBS:	F**king hell! Aislaby, Thornton, TSV Eltingen.
PRESENT CLUB:	None.
INTERNATIONAL HONOURS:	International honours? None. Tiddlywinks champion. Playing for TSV Eltingen.
DALE DEBUT:	Oooh hell I don't know. Well it's years ago!
MOST MEMORABLE GAME:	What you on about now?
MOST MEMORABLE GOAL:	F**k off Lee Sharpe, has he ever scored a goal? Andy Hill's when it hit his nose and went in!
BEST PLAYER SEEN:	Who isn't? It could be, it isn't, that Derby player this year I think.
BEST MANAGER:	Howard Wilkinson
BEST LEEDS PLAYER:	Batty, Batty aye.
FAV. OTHER TEAM:	None. Oh, Rangers, it's only other team I like.
FAVOURITE CAR:	Well, Jags I think. Any what goes really.
FAV. BAKED BEANS:	All what make you fart.
FAV. TOMATO SOUP:	Oh I don't know.
FAV. BROWN SAUCE:	Haven't got a clue.
FAVOURITE FOOD:	Oh well that's impossible, I like that so much, I'm just a gannet!
FAVOURITE DRINK:	Beer, any beer.
BEST FRIEND:	I don't know really, right hand never tires.
HAVE YOU GOT ANY CATS?	No
FAV. TV SHOW:	F**king hell, I haven't got a favourite one. Blue movies.
FAV. GREEK RESTAURANT:	Favourite what? Where do you get a f**king Greek Restaurant from round here!
FAV. SUPERSTORE:	Super...F**king hell I don't know.
MOST MEMORABLE SUPERNATURAL EXPERIENCE:	What? Lasting all night in Thailand
DO YOU KNOW ANY ALIENS?	Andy Hill. I don't know really
BEST PLANET VISITED:	Daft cunt, there is only one! Mars. When I was on Speed in Germany, I was floating, f**king on the clouds man, floating man...
FAV. BREED OF SHEEP:	Don't know really. One on a plate
FAVOURITE OPERA:	I hate f**king opera. Can't stand them yowling b**tards!
FAV. CLIFF RICHARD SONG:	F**king hell none, he's a puff!
MOST MARS BARS EATEN IN ONE DAY:	I don't know, how the hell do I know
WHAT IS YOUR ANSWER TO THE CURRENT PROBLEMS FACING TDFC?	What's my what? Oh, sack the managers. Barnes and Aconley out!

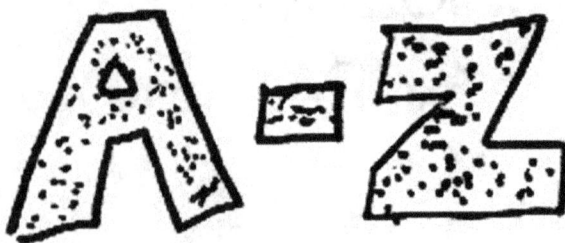 **OF THE DALE**

A is for awful, which Dale were last season

B is for Barney - the Dale boss and a brick shithouse in the centre of defence. It is also for bald which is what Eddie is.

C is for crap - the word which has appeared most frequently in 'The Escaped Horse'.

D is for dirty bugger - which is what Steve Avison was before leaving the club.

E is for 'Escaped Horse'. A nice easy one there, eh?

F is for fit - which is what we go into when Dale score.

G is for Ganton - which is where we will be playing next season. See you there.

H is for Hill. We've got two hills - Stuart and Randy. Come to think of it, so has Maria Whittaker. (Ho ho)

I is for Ipswich. Somewhere we didn't play last season. (Well what else starts with I?)

J is for jukebox. If we had one, Randy Thrill would always have the Waterboys on, and Andy Johnson would keep playing the Carpenters. Perhaps we'd better not...

K is for kick - see 'd' for further details.

L is for lose - Dale did it 12 times last season.

M is for management - which is what we haven't got.

N is for nothing, which is what we ended up with last season. It is also for nuke, which we often feel like doing to Bridlington because Mermaid and RBL both come from there.

O is for old - which is what Raymond Smith definitely is.

P is for psycho - see Sean Dixon for further details.

Q is for Queens Park Rangers. We borrowed an idea from a QPR fanzine in an earlier edition.

R is for Randy Thrill - most slagged off player and window cleaner extraordinaire.

S is for sex - which we've discovered is the most important thing in most of your minds.

T is for third - which we used to come very often in the good 'ol days...

continued on next page....

U is for useless. It speaks for itself really.

V is for God. Well, Victor Welburn really, but it's the same thing.

W is for Will Balderson, official Escaped Horse player of the year 1990/1. An accolade he'll treasure for the rest of his life.

X is for a score draw on the pools coupon. Dale had three score draws last season. (And you thought we wouldn't think of anything for X. We're just great, aren't we?)

Y is for youth. Dale have four - Lee Brackstone, Deany Rick, Julian Bevan and Raymond Smith. Ho ho.

Z is for Zebadee - star of the 'Magic Rounabout'. Dale were definitely not magic last season.

++

FROM THE ARCHIVES

1906 UNBELIEVABLE SHOCK WORLD EXCLUSIVE

When you turn the page you will gape in amazement. You will stare at the writing in front of you and think, 'surely not!' But your eyes are not deceiving you. God is not playing a silly trick, and no, it isn't a hoax. Over the page there is a photocopied page from a 'Parish magazine' – from 1906. (Yes, nineteennoughtsix) In the bottom right hand corner there is something about Dale's annual dinner. We can just imagine Shep and Thrill dancing at the recent piss-up, and what was a 'farce'? Anyway, how did we get this sensational world-gasping exclusive? We borrowed loads of these mags from the Vicar (ask him if you want) and scanned through them all to get anything about Dale FC. Unfortuneately this is all we could find (Ashley Welburn wasn't around then to send details in) although there was quite a bit about the cricket team. We know you'll be amazed by the 'Escaped Horse reference department, and you'll be stunned and moved by what we go through for you. It'll have brought you close to tears – but don't worry, we won't publish an exclusive on you if we find you blubbering in the streets – this time, we understand. And all this for a tiny amount, all of which is given back to help our beloved little Thornton Dale Football Club. Next time you pull on a Dale shirt, wear it with pride and passion – remember your loyal band of supporters who'll follow you to the ends of the earth – remember what they do every fortnight, how much pain and anguish, sweat, toil and tears they lose when producing this sacred journal. We must stop now, we're running out of Kleenex. Sob, sob...

THORNTON DALE

AND

ELLERBURNE-with-WILTON

PARISH MAGAZINE

Vol. XIX.—No. 4.   APRIL, 1906.   Price

THORNTON CHURCH.

SERVICES—SUNDAY—10·30 a.m. and 6·30 p.m. On First Sunday
at 2 p.m.

Holy Baptism on the First Sunday in the Month at 2·15 p.m

Holy Communion on the First and Third Sundays in the Month a
Prayer. On other Sundays at 8·0 a.m.

SUNDAY SCHOOL—9·45 a.m. and 2 p.m. There is a Library at

Sunday School.

ELLERBURNE PARISH CHURCH.

SERVICES.—SUNDAY—Morning Service, with Holy Communion last S
month, and on Easter Day, Christmas Day, and Whit
at 10·30 a.m.;

Afternoon (during Winter Months) 2·30 p.m.; Evening 6·30 p.m.

WILTON CHURCH.

SUNDAY—Morning, 10·30 a.m.   Afternoon, 2·30 p.m. (when there is M
at Ellerburne).   Holy Communion first Sunday in the mon

BAPTISM

Feb. 23: (privately), Doris, daughter of Henry and Barbara
Wood, Thornton Marishes.

BURIALS

Feb. 1: Mary Storr, aged 85 years.
" 17: Margaret Burnell, aged 85 years
" 20: Annie Elizabeth Dale, aged 1 month.

CALENDAR.

			Service	
Wednesday, March 7	Ember Days.		7·0 p.m.
Friday	"	9	"	10·30 a.m.
Saturday	"	10	"	6·0 p.m.
Tuesday	"	20	Bishop of Beverley.	11·30 a.m.
	Confirmation		

There will be Lenten Services on—

Wednesdays, March 7, 14, 21 .. .. .. 7·0 p.m.
Fridays March 30, April 6 .. .. ..

On Wednesday, March 28, it is proposed to
have a Jumble Sale, in aid of the Organ fund, to
take place in the Grammar School, from 4·0 to
8·0 p.m. Any contributions will be gladly
received by Miss Heslop and Miss K. Hill.

The Clothing Club has been resumed and is
open weekly on Mondays at the National School,
at 3·30 p.m.

The Sewing party for the Sale of Work fund
are invited to meet at the Rectory on Thursdays,
at 2·15.

Miss N. Hayward has left the school staff to
take a similar position as assistant mistress at
Old Malton. We shall miss her as well in the
Sunday School, where her help has always been
freely given. The vacancy will be filled by Miss
M. Hardy, who comes luck to us with excellent
testimonials from the school at Hackness.

A concert promoted by the Football Club took
place on Feb. 16. It consisted of a mixed programme, followed by a farce, which went very
well, and caused considerable amusement. The
programme concluded with a dance. The Committee of the Club wish to thank all who in any
way contributed to the success of the entertain-
ment, through which the Club funds have
benefited to the amount of £6. The season has
been a fairly successful one—matches won 6,
drawn 4, lost 3.

BAPTISM.

Feb. 7: (privately), Annie Elizabeth, daughter of Laurence
and Esther Jane Dale, Hagg Farm

BURIAL

Feb. 3: Arthur Donald Medcalf, Whitbygate, aged 22 ye

THE CATECHISM.

The Catechism naturally divides itself into fi
sections.

1. Exposition of the Baptismal Covenant.
2. The Creed and its explanation.
3. The Ten Commandments and their explanation.
4. The Lord's Prayer and its explanation.
5. The doctrine of the Sacraments.

I. *Exposition of the Baptismal Covenant.*

The reader must bear in mind that the whol
of the Baptismal Covenant starts from the child
knowledge of his Baptismal adoption in Chris
because of his Christian name.

The Scriptural idea of a Covenant with Go
begins with God's blessings actually given t
man. And then when man has understood th
Covenant, there is the corresponding duty t
God. So in the Baptismal Covenant, it teach
the child simply to accept with thankfulness h
share in the Christian Covenant, as given him t
the call of God, and to pray that he may continu
to be in that Covenant.

It is well to note here that the Baptism
Blessings begins with the personal relation
the child to Christ as a "*member of Him*"—see
Corinthians xii 27.—Now ye are the body
Christ, and members in particular." That is,
having that close individual unity with Hi
which is frequently strengthened by such passag
of Holy Scripture as follows :—St. John xv.
"I am the vine, ye are the branches.," Galatio
iii. 27. "For as many of you as have be
baptized into Christ have put on Christ." A
then being a ' member of Him', there follows t
other relations to "God and man ; namely, t
"Sonship to God" by adoption in His So
Romans viii 14—" For as many as are led
the Spirit of God, they are the sons of Go
And the " inheritance," that is, participation in
present and future—" of the Kingdom of Heave

In and through all there is an appeal to t
Spirit of Love, love to the Saviour, love to t
Father, love to all) as brethren in His family.

DULL SPORTS OF THE DALE

NUMBER 1 : SNOOKER

SNOOKER FINAL TABLES 1990/1

DIVISION A	PLD	W	D	L	PTS	DIVISION B	PLD	W	D	L	PTS
THORNTON DALE C	24	15	7	2	91	Bright Steels F	22	15	6	1	89
Pickering Cons B	24	15	6	3	88	Bright Steels C	22	14	6	2	81
Bright Steels E	24	14	8	2	88	Bright Steels B	22	14	2	6	78
Pickering Cons A	24	14	4	6	83	THORNTON DALE A	22	10	7	5	77
Norton Cons C	24	11	7	6	79	MBFC A	22	8	9	5	71
Malton Cons B	24	9	10	5	77	BRSA B	22	9	3	10	65
BRSA C	24	8	9	7	75	Pickering Cons C	22	8	6	8	65
Malton Cons A	24	5	9	10	72	Norton Cons B	22	7	4	11	60
Malton Cons D	24	4	8	12	62	British League C	22	5	7	10	60
British Legion	23	7	5	11	61	Malton Cons C	22	4	7	11	56
Pickering WMC	24	5	6	13	61	Knapton Silo	22	5	4	13	50
Bright Steels A	24	3	6	15	49	MBFC B	22	1	3	18	40
Malton Squash	23	0	5	18	42						

Well, what can we say? At least someone in the village was successful last year! How come the 'C' team beat the 'A' team, though? And where the hell are the 'B' team? Looking elsewhere, there's loads of 'Cons' around. Perhaps these are 'convicts' or more likely Conservative clubs. But if these are Conservatives, where are the 'Malton Liberal Democrats', the 'Norton Labours' or the Goathland Monster Raving Loonies?

'BRSA' are obviously reference to out famous fans, the initials spelling out 'Big Rampant Shaun Aconley' or even 'Boring Rocker Steven Allardice'. Pickering Working Mens' Club obviously didn't work very hard, or perhaps that's because they're really 'Pickering Womens' marmalade Club'? And it's no suprise Malton Squash did so crap - they weren't even playing the right sport!

Into division B and Bright Steels certainly shone out. (Ho ho). Our A team can be seen just behind them and Mick Barnes gets into the act with his club MBFC, or Mick Barnes Football Club. Shaun or Steven are at it again and what about British League? Is it a famous Gazette misprint that should read 'British Legion' or have the top clubs already broke away and formed a 'Super League', as they have threatened to do? We should be told. Knapton Silo - what a lovely name for a snooker club, and in true Barney fashion, a team with his initials finishes bottom!

SNEB AT THE SNOOKER TABLE...

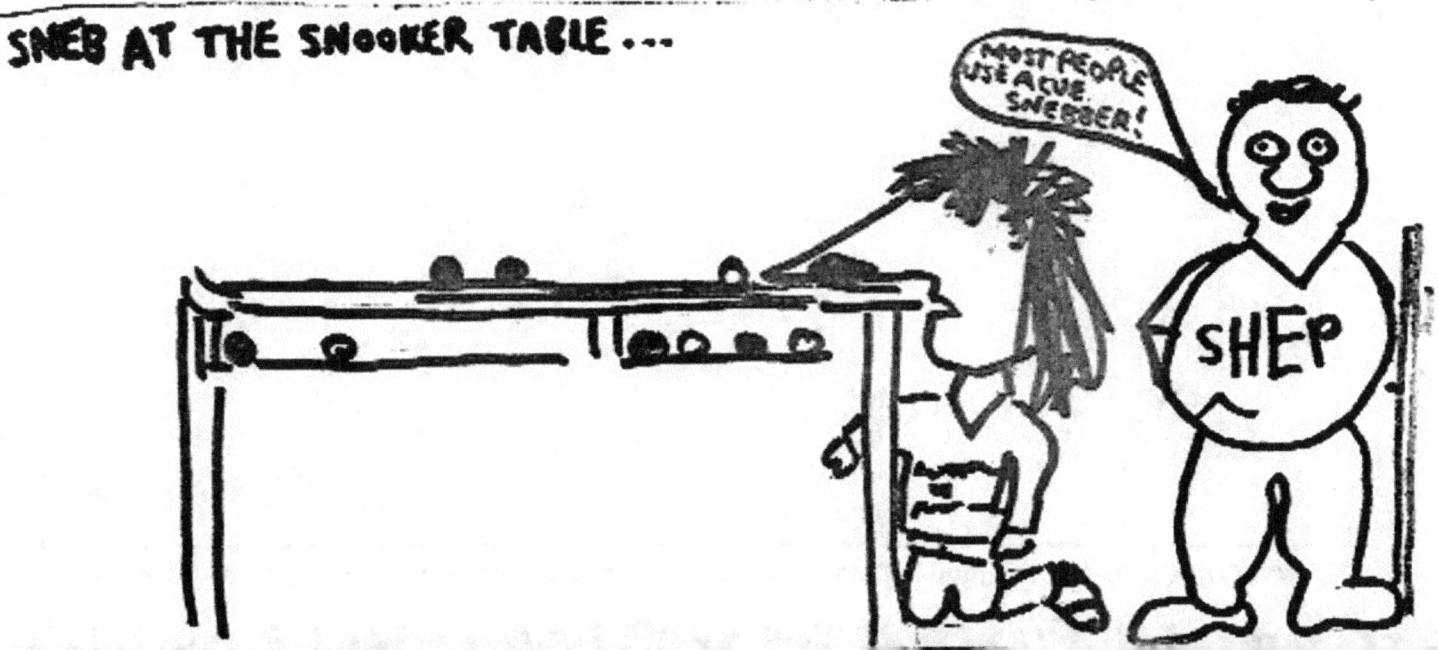

'BESTY, BESTY WHAT'S THE SCORE?"

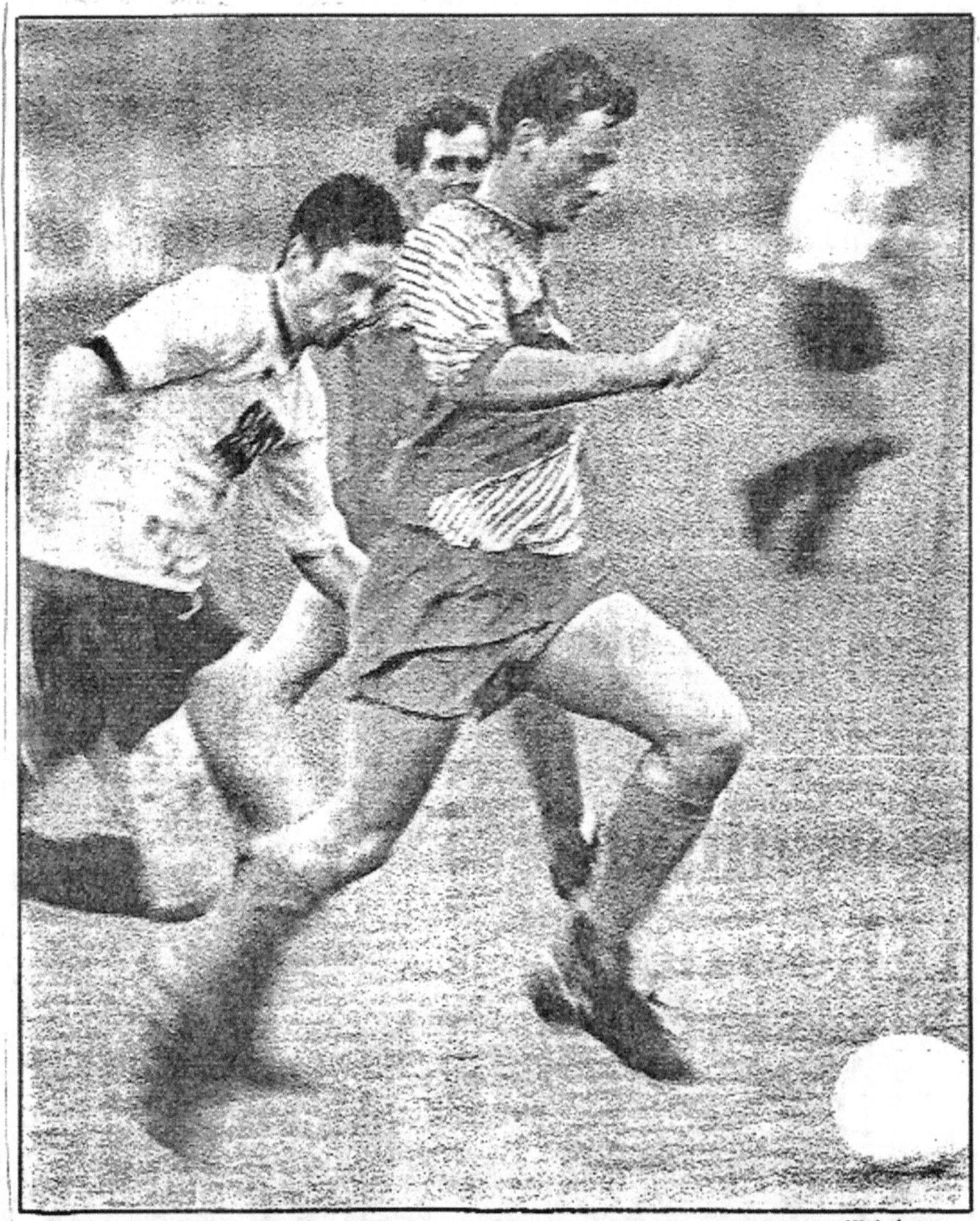

WYKEHAM ATTACK: Thornton-le-Dale were made to battle hard for their 1-0 victory over Wykeham

FH PLAYER OF THE YEAR 1990/1 - WILL BALDERSON

THE ESCAPED HORSE

WHO'S WHO

A DEFINITIVE GUIDE TO EVERYONE WHO HAS EVER APPEARED IN THE PREVIOUS 15 EDITIONS OF 'THE ESCAPED HORSE'

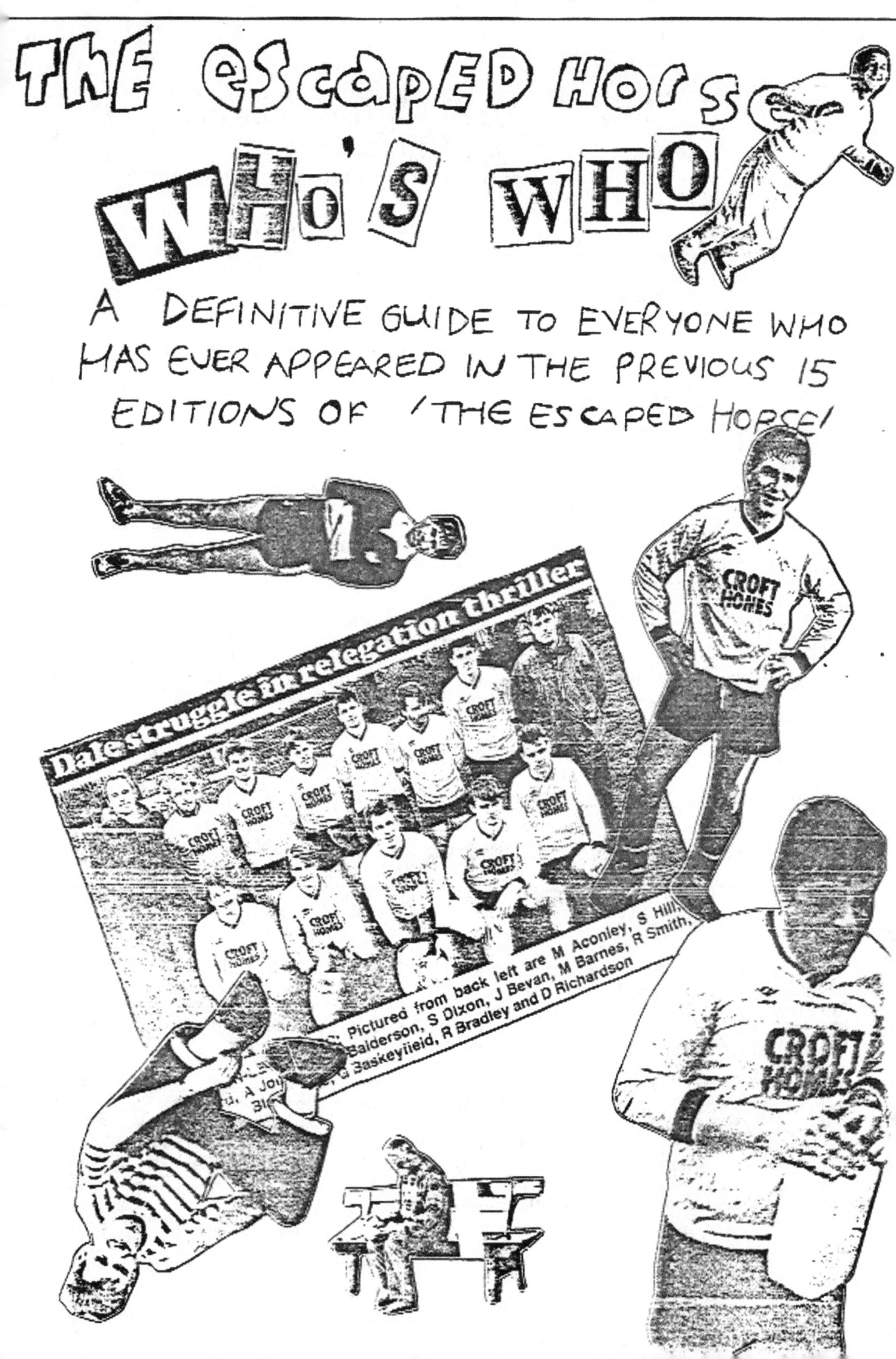

Dale struggle in relegation thriller

Pictured from back left are M Aconley, S Hill, Balderson, S Dixon, J Bevan, M Barnes, R Smith, Baskeyfield, R Bradley and D Richardson

Well, after two years in the high life enjoying numerous round the world cruises, fast cars and loose women, we've finally exhausted all the profits that we'd made from the previous 15 issues of THE ESCAPED HORSE. There's only one thing for it then, isn't there? Yes, that's right. Another edition, if only to replenish the coffers in time for next month's scheduled trip to Haiti.

This literary gem will transport you back to the halcyon days of the late eighties. You can relive the unhappy times with the, well, the slightly less unhappy times. It will allow you to remember the stories and most importantly the people who made Thornton Dale Football Club what it is today. A laughing stock.

****

Oops, nearly forgot - back issues. We recently found a whole bundle of them in the Escaped Horse offices underneath piles and piles of dirty Indian Takeaway trays and empty cans of Tartan Special. Never ones to miss a commercial opportunity we dusted them off, sellotaped them back together and can now offer you issue numbers 15, 12, 11, 10, 9 and 8 for the outlandishly cheap price of 20p each. Should you require our Reserve Team Special or any of the issues not mentioned above, they will cost about a quid each because we will have to reprint them. Except issue one, which despite only consisting of one page will cost a fiver. (Well everyone else flogs off their first edition for a hugely inflated price, so why shouldn't we?)

If you're outside the area (TEH goes worldwide these days, you know) you can write to Church Farm House, High Street, Thornton Dale, Pickering, N.YORKS YO18 7QW with your money and your comments. Please be as honest as you like - it doesn't matter to us what you think. All that it means is that if you're not very complimentary we'll come round to your house and smash your face in.

****

So then. Turn El Dorado off, grab a few crates of beer, lock up yer daughters and let's go!

THE ESCAPED HORSE BIBLIOGRAPHY

MAURICE ACONLEY: This man is Mr Thornton Dale FC. You name it, he does it. Well, except writing this fanzine. And playing. And...oh, forget it.

MIKE ACONLEY: Took over the managerial reins in the mid eighties and promptly transformed Dale from a side on the verge of promotion to a side teetering on the brink of relegation. Realising he wasn't too good at it he eventually ran off with some bird and - voila! Dale suddenly have their best season for years. Pure coincidence, of course.

SHAUN ACONLEY: Young Dale supporter and son of the above, who had a strange penchant for climbing trees and playing hide and seek while games were in progress. Thus we often had the scenario where, as Dale threw everyone forward in a last gasp bid to equalise in a vital Cup game, just as tension reached fever pitch, the nerve jangling silence would be shattered by jubilant cries of "I've found you, I've found you! Come out! Come out! from the adjoining field.

BILLY ATKINSON: Flicking through our back issues, we can only find one mention of him - limping off during a painful defeat at Barrowcliff. So we're a bit flummoxed as to what to write. We know he had blonde hair and...erm...that he limped off once at Barrowcliff.

EDDIE AVISON: Veteran midfielder with no hair. We can't really think of anything else to say about him. Crap. There, how's that?

EDDIE AVISON'S DAD: Leapt to stardom when The Escaped Horse revealed his monstrous past playing record for the Dale. Overnight he changed from a Burgess Feeds worker into a world reknowned celebrity who was forever jetting off to all corners of the globe for autograph sessions and film parts. And what a load of bollocks we've just written.

STEVE AVISON: A modern version of the above, except that he didn't go globetrotting. Even if we'd wanted him to we probably couldn't have found him because half the time he just walked off the pitch and went home in the middle of a vital Third Division promotion (or relegation if we're talking about the Mike Aconley era) tussle.

MARK BAGNEL: Joined towards the end of the Escaped Horse's lifespan so we don't really remember that much about him, except that he looked remarkably like Feargal Sharkey. Come to think of it, it could have been Feargal Sharkey playing under a pseud...psudon...different name. That's made us feel all nostalgic now - do you remember Feargal Sharkey, with his catchy poppy tunes and his husky Irish voice? Why don't you send in your memories of him and we'll bring out a Feargal Sharkey special?

WILL BALDERSON: A real rock in the centre of our defence. Unfortunately he resembled that sticky pink seaside type - ie. he dissolved when the opposition started to show their teeth. Even so, he won the prestigious Escaped Horse Player of the Year Trophy once, which says a lot for the rest of the team.

MICK BARNES: This loyal player manager took over after the Mike Aconley regime and led the club out from under the black clouds - and into a thunderstorm. No, actually he didn't, we're just in the mood for slagging everybody off. Has brought a lot of youngsters into the club but often cancels out the teenage effect by including himself in the team and sending the average age rocketing up towards the three figure mark. Loved it once when the fanzine labelled him a 'Brick Shithouse in the centre of our defence'. With retrospect, if you take away the 'brick' and the 'house' we think you'll be nearer the mark.

GLENN BASKEYFIELD: A top young teenage striker who shunned offers from the big English clubs and instead opted for a trial with Leeds United. Somehow or other he failed to win a contract there and upon his return to the Dale yellow he struggled to revert back to the higher standard of soccer at the Greyhound Ground. Eventually he drifted away citing some pitiful excuse about university or something as reason for his departure.

BRIAN BEST: Much loved by the Dale faithful before his shock transfer to deadly rivals Wykeham. Instantly he was transformed into a figure of hatred who had his car set on fire and his house ransacked by crazed fans. (Well, he didn't but just let it be a warning. Oops - do you think we ought to delete that last sentence in case the police come round?) Anyway, back to Brian Best. Ah yes. There was dancing in the streets when Wykeham visited Dale for two Cup games in the space of seven days soon after his transfer and we TOTALLY AND UTTERLY GUBBED THEM

-

TWICE! - 1-0 and 2-1. Brian Best was too embarassed to appear at the Greyhound Ground ever again. Except to walk his dogs early in the morning when no one was about.

JULIAN BEVAN: Another University hungry teenager who only played for one season but made such an impression in defence that he swept to the ultimate accolade of Escaped Horse Player of the Year. Now we've got to think of something bad to say about him...erm...he was tall and thin.

DEGGY BOND: Incredible older supporter who turned up to most home games in his yellow chevette (do you remember chevette's? Why don't you send in your memories of them and we can bring out a Chevette special?) and proceeded to slag off everyone and anyone for the following 90 minutes. Except us who, being young and innocent, were spared from his abuse and instead indoctrinated by his foul language. Thus we were nearly ejected from the ground on numerous occasions for calling refs and goalkeepers 'shitheads', 'wankers' et al. We didn't quite go as far as hitting the opposing team's captain like he did, though.

LEE BRACKSTONE: Lee played for half a season but his silky skills were wasted on the boggy Scarborough and District League pitches and he soon faded away into anonymity. That's right - he was put in our midfield. Occasionally he came back to attention when his dad yelled various tactical phrases at him from the touchline. Those, too, were wasted on Scarborough and District League pitches as the vast majority of players didn't even know what a pass was, let alone a corner or a goal kick.

RICHARD BRADLEY: Quite a good, flying winger whose career was tragically cut short when he began to play too well too often. The team went to desperate lengths to be rid of him - once they even sent him into the shop for some crisps on the way to an away game, and when he returned to the roadside he found that they had all sodded off and left him.

RAY COOK: Like Billy Atkinson, we can only find one reference to him in the fanzines, and can't for the life of us remember who he was. We think he was bald, and he was definitely a psycho because the reference to him says 'Psycho Ray Cook'.

DEREK COULSON: Frequented the Greyhound Ground during the Escaped Horse's very early days, but the one vivid memory we have of 'Big Der', as we never called him, was of him kicking the shit out of some Mermaid defender on the goal line during one particularly stormy game with our friends from Bridlington. He also bought a copy of the Escaped Horse in the pub on one of the presentation evenings.

SEAN DIXON: Apparently he's still kicking around in a Dale shirt, so we'd better be careful what we say. Probably the only reason why he's still going is that he's banged all the opposing players into the ground by now. The views expressed in this fanzine are not necessarily those of the editors.

ANDY HILL: We're getting on reasonably well with Mr Hill these days (yes, we're down to just one dose of verbal abusage each day) so we don't really think it would be wise to reopen old wounds. But we're still going to. He was the main target of all the Escaped Horse taunts - very unfairly because, with retrospect, his hair isn't untidy and his nose isn't big - and we had a few brushes with death as the man himself gave chase to us on numerous occasions after some particularly hard hitting stories. Happily we survived and we're going to take this opportunity to get our own back now - YOU BIG NOSED UNTIDY STARK RAVING MAD HIPPO!

KENNY HILL: Andy's brother, who occasionally turned up to watch matches with a huge dog by his side. And a hairy, four legged beast too. He did actually play a couple of times, not that we remember anything about his performances. Let's clutch at straws and say he was crap.

STUART HILL: Long serving goalkeeper who finally came to his senses a couple of seasons ago and left the club to join the world acclaimed Pigeon Pie FC of Sherburn. We very much hate to admit it, but he was good. At this point we would usually make some joke about him living on a farm, ie. by calling him a sheep shagger or something, but we're too mature to do that these days, so we won't.

RALPH INGLEBY: Ralphie didn't actually have anything at all to do with TDFC (Tell a lie - he once went to a pre season training session and fell over doing a backward somersault. Oh yes, and he came to a game and sold us some Leeds United Christmas Draw tickets aswell once. We never won, the bastard) but he made his way into virtually every issue of the fanzine due to his strange Leeds supporting tendencies and, of course, his hatred for us editors. He also featured in perhaps the best ever article - that interview he did in issue 15. Oh, and that leads us on quite nicely to a reminder that back issues are still available from the Escaped Horse address at only 20p each plus postage. Two for 40p. Bargain or what - they're practically collectors' items now you know.

ANDY JOHNSON: Another flying, silky skilled winger in the Richard Bradley/Lee Brackstone/Totally shite mode who scored the odd goal now and again and...erm...flew down the wing silky skilledly occasionally too, I suppose. (What what do you expect me to write? It's half past bloody midnight, I'm totally knackered and the other editors have gone to bed. Hence the sudden change to the singular 'I' instead of the plural 'We', by the way)

GEORGE REVELEY: A quite extraordinary referee whose infrequent visits to the Greyhound Ground almost inevitably resulted in a mass brawl and a mass of early baths (a figure of speech - we don't actually have a bath, unless you count the rusty one that they use as a horse's drinking trough behind the stand, of course).

DEAN RICHARDSON: Yet another student, and yet another to get his big chance thank's to Mick Barnes' policy of selecting players from the youth team stable. Stable, in fact, is the correct word because he was a right carthorse. In fact, that's being cruel to carthorses. He was absolutely, totally, unbelievably, mind bendingly USELESS. Thank God he buggered off to University. Hope to God he's not reading this. The views expressed in this fanzine etc etc

RAYMOND SMITH: Yet another to get his big chance thanks to Mick Barnes' policy of selecting players from the youth team stable. Ho ho. I like a bit of contradiction these days, don't you?

MARK SHEPHERD: Another member of that elite group of starlets who received more than their fair share of ribbing from the Escaped Horse. Not surprising really because he was such a fat bastard. Oops no, I didn't mean that. I see him every day, you see. Anyway, enough of the personal vendetta's, we seem to have been forgetting about the football over these last few pen pics, so let's get back to the main point of this fanzine - a celebration of Thornton Dale FC's footballing prowess. Mark Shepherd's footballing ability, then. Ahem...

RICHARD THORNER: A hard, tough central defender very much in the 'Steve Avison' mould. Again he was another of these awkward bastards whose Dale career was at its nadir (God knows what that means but it sounds ace, doesn't it?) just as the Escaped Horse was getting going, but we do remember one match at Ryedale a few years ago. Sitting comfortably? Let us elaborate. (We've bloody well got to because we've only filled 5 pages so far and we're getting dangerously near to the letter 'Z'). Ryedale are pinning Dale back in their own half so, obviously, our strikers are loitering around doing nothing on the half way line (as opposed to loitering around doing nothing in the opponents' penalty area). Richard Thorner, long since departed from the club, is watching from the sidelines and for some reason harbours a particular dislike for one of our aforementioned goal poachers. He plucks up the courage to shout an odd personal remark at him. All seems well. But then, after a split second of silence and completely without warning, our star man wakens from his slumber, races to the touchline with a speed never witnessed before by the Dale fans and bashes the bemused Mr Thorner over the head, knocking him the floor. He then turns, returns to the centre circle, and goes back to sleep. Like I'm going to do now. Goodnight. God bless.

NICK VERMONT: Ah. Morning - did you sleep well? That's good. Right then - Nick Vermont. Played a few games but then, though still registered with the club, just vanished without trace. He's never been seen since. Have YOU seen him? If so, you could qualify for a community action trust reward.

ASHLEY WELBURN: I was going to start with the sentence, 'This man is Mr Thornton Dale FC' but then I glanced at the letter 'A's and realised I'd already said that about Maurice Aconley. Oh damn. Suffice to say that he does everything that Maurice doesn't do, and that they overlap a bit. He even used to play - for the Reserve team, may they rest in peace, and he wrote a couple of poems for The Escaped Horse when it was going through its romantic period.

VICTOR WELBURN: The second Welburn who, quite remarkably, has a brother called Ashley. Incredible isn't it? Victor carried on playing for a bit longer and quickly became a cult figure with the Dale faithful because of his red headband and his displays of dazzling incompetence. Sorry Vic, we didn't mean that - we just had to keep up with the tradition, you know. Had a comic named after him, by the way. (Oh yes, and another thing - the other editors have rejoined the fray, which explains our quick return to the plural 'we'. There's no such thing as a syntax error at Escaped Horse Towers, you know,

OTHER FAMOUS NAMES WHO HAVE HAD THE PRIVILEGE OF BEING MENTIONED IN PREVIOUS EDITIONS OF THE ESCAPED HORSE, ACCORDING TO THIS LIST THAT WE MADE YEARS AGO AND FORGOT ABOUT:

GARY LINEKER AND DAVID HOWELLS: A delerious vote of thanks to them in issue two for scoring against Leeds. We had to stop this trend later on as Leeds got worse and worse and the 'vote of thanks' began to take up half of the magazine.

TEENAGE MUTANT HERO TURTLES: We don't have a clue why and quite frankly we can't be arsed to dig through the back issues to find out because the pubs open soon and we're thirsty.

STEFFI GRAF: A sort of grovelling apology to Andy Hill in the form of 'Steffi Graf has a bigger nose than him'. Bet that made him feel better.

KEN DODD: See 'Teenage Mutant Hero Turtles.

FEARGAL SHARKEY: Obviously connected to the star's Dale double, Mark Bagnel. By the way, has anyone dredged up any memories of the great man yet? We're still waiting for your call.

NICOLE: Sounds like a porn star or someone. Probably was, come to think of it. Oh yes, we remember...

IRAQ/TORIES: The Gulf War was raging and The Escaped Horse felt the time was right to venture into politics. Hence the mandatory fanzine 'Ins and Outs' list and, well, Iraq and the Tories appearing on it.

PETER NICHOLAS: That Chelsea player. We had some room at the bottom of a·page so we just stuck a panini sticker of him there.

GRAEME SOUNESS/HOWARD WILKINSON/LEE SHARPE: Various references to, sensationally enough, famous players and managers. Christ this is getting boring.

ZEBADEE: Another essential fanzine feature, the A-Z. We didn't have anything else for 'Z', ok?

MARIA WHITTAKER: Bet you can't guess what context we used her in. Oh, the joys of youth.

****

Right, well then. That's about it. Is wasn't too painful was it? Now we're left with the slight problem of how we're going to fill the remaining page and a half. Erm... Perhaps we can just carry on writing space filling sentences like the one you're reading now? Or maybe we could use larger type fonts to take up more room? Or even stick in some totally irrelevant photographs like these:

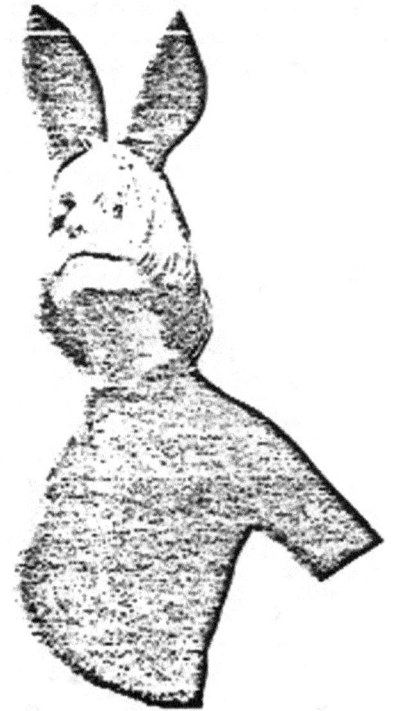
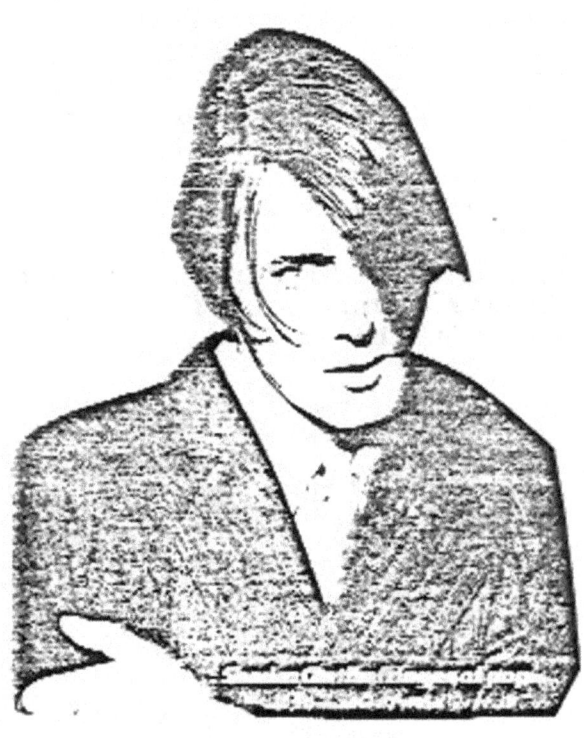

THE ESCAPED QUOTES

Undoubtedly everyone's favourite feature in THE ESCAPED HORSE was the 'Quotes of the Week' section which appeared at the bottom of the last page in every issue. This can probably be explained by the fact that it usually only took up two or three lines but never mind, we've painstakingly waded through all our back issues and can now bring to you

DALE QUOTES: AN ANTHOLOGY

(the thesaurus is working overtime here!)

"Oh, you're crap you lot!" - Brian Best
"His nose isn't big, it just grows when he lies" - Ralph about Andy Hill
"You can get a Mirror for that" - Stuart Hill about the price of TEH
"Shep would be a lot better if he lost two stone" - Dean Richardson
"Your fanzine's crap, it doesn't have enough swearing" - Shaun Aconley
"Is thee simple?" - Eddie Avison
"Oh, you're crap you lot!" - Brian Best
"Bevan is a big dog's cock" - Andy Hill
"Shep eats too many cherries" (?) - Craig Barnes
"There's no difference between 10-0 or 1-0" - Brian Best
"Our keeper gave up after a couple" - Brian Best
"I fair clogged him one" - Deggy Bond about the time he hit a Mermaid player
"Oh, you're crap you lot!" - Brian Best
"I'm knackered" - Mick Barnes
"1991 is Dale's year - the year of the donkeys" - Mick Barnes
"Sheffield United have got more points than us" - Andy Johnson
"Who needs a tracksuit when you've got a boilersuit" - Eddie Avison
"Thirty pence, bloody hell!" - Richard Bradley
"Oh, you're crap you lot!" - Brian Best
"Dean can't take his ale" - Lee Brackstone
"Scum!" - Brian Best
"Besty scored two? Bloody hell!" - Victor Welburn
"Run past me and I'll shag yer" - Plaxtons player to Dean Richardson
"They're not doing so well this year. Mick Barnes says it's because they get tired chasing after all the women" - Anonymous in Garbuts shop
"Oh, you're crap you lot!" - Brian Best
"I know I'm fat but you don't have to go on about it" - Mark Shepherd
"Is this where the shindig is?" - Victor Welburn on presentations night
"Mad bastards" - Aislaby United keeper to bemused Dale fans behind goal
"Daft cunts" - North Cliff keeper to bemused Dale fans behind goal
"Shut your f**king gobs and f**k off" - Kirkbymoorside Reserves keeper to bemused Dale fans behind goal
"Oh, you're crap you lot!" - Brian Best

****

Now we'd better finish with some more irrelevant photographs, just so the outside cover looks attractive to any prospective buyers who may glance at it in the shop:

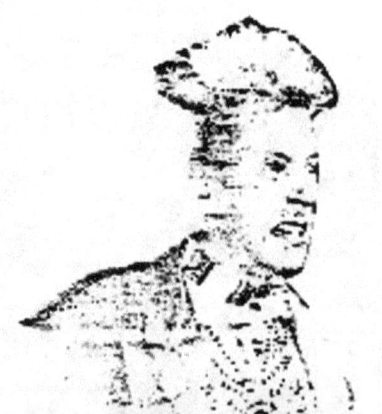

TWENTY FOUR NIL!

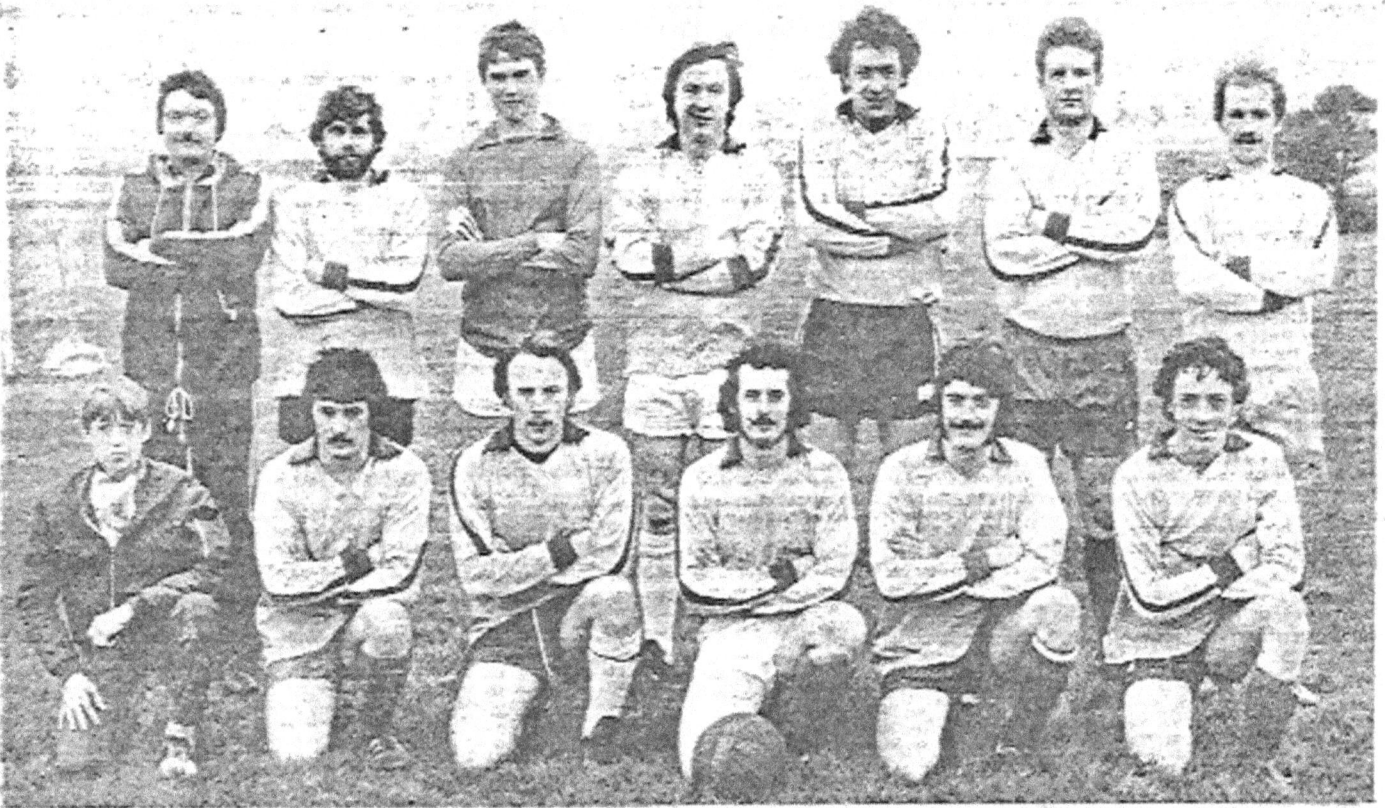

PAGE 48—The Mercury, Saturday 13 November 1982

MERCURY SPORT — 3

Beckett League side Thornton Dale (left to right, back): A. Welburn (player-manager), J. Abbey, M. Anson, G. Hunt, S. Stead, B. Longbone, A. Geary; front, R. Thorner (sub), S. Hill, A. White, M. Downing, V. Welburn, and L. Welburn.

DALE RESERVES

1982-1985 : AN ALMOST COMPLETE RECORD

1982/3

5 SEP: DALE 4 BAGBY & BALK 3. This game heralded the rebirth of the Reserves after a two year break. They entertained Bagby & Balk, making their first appearance in the Beckett League. The accident prone visitors won't have forgotten that game very easily. As the team met, one of the players was injured as he got into his car. He was unable to make the trip. They started the game with ten men, but after 10 minutes lost another man with a broken leg. Dale were 4-1 up with 15 minutes left, goals from Derek Coulson (2), John Abbey and Peter Hill, but Bagby fought back and almost snatched a point.

12 SEP: COXWOLD 13 DALE 1. Victor Welburn grabbed the consolation goal for battling Dale.

26 SEP: FARNDALE 2 DALE 4. John Abbey was Dale's four goal hero.

3 OCT: DALE 0 HOVINGHAM 6. Dale held on for the first half hour.

10 OCT: AMPLEFORTH 1 DALE 3. Referee Matt Fenwick praised both sides for their sportsmanship. Brian Longbone and John Abbey cancelled out the home side's early strike, Abbey's goal a sensational 20 yarder. Late on, Longbone grabbed his second in his comeback game for Dale.

17 OCT: WESTLERS RESERVES 7 DALE 3. Westlers led 5-1 at half time, prolific marksman John Abbey having scored for Dale. Abbey scored again in the second half and it was a great day for Les Welburn who scored his first ever goal in a Dale jersey.

24 OCT: DALE 2 TERRINGTON 4. John Abbey and Les Welburn were on the mark again, while Steve Stead produced a man of the match winning display.

31 OCT: DALE 1 WESTLERS RESERVES 9. Steve Stead was the scorer, Mike Downing was outstanding and our defence was crap again.

7 NOV: GILLAMOOR 3 DALE 1. A much improved performance from Dale but even the return of Adrian Geary in midfield couldn't prevent another defeat. John Abbey scored from the spot for Dale.

14 NOV: DALE 2 KIRKBYMOORSIDE RESERVES 3. Dale were three down after 12 minutes and it should have been more but for Mike Avison in goal. Dale were a new team in the second half and they roared back through John Abbey and Brian Longbone. Abbey missed an easy opportunity to snatch a point in the dying seconds.

28 NOV: KIRKDALE UNITED 4 DALE 5. Goals from Brian Longbone and Ashley White twice gave Dale the lead but Kirkdale stormed bak to lead 4-2 at half time. However Dale never know when to give up and in the second half, player manager Ashley Welburn set up John Abbey. Longbone equalised and sub Ian Holmes rounded things off in style with seconds to spare.

9 DEC: DALE 1 KIRKDALE UNITED 1. All square in this Hospital Cup tie.

12 DEC: HOVINGHAM 10 DALE 1. A pretty bad performance from Dale.

19 DEC: DALE 1 ROSEDALE 3. Hot shot striker Brian Longbone scored against his old club.

26 DEC: KIRKBYMOORSIDE RESERVES 11 DALE 4. With Dale doing all that attacking they forgot about their defence and allowed Kirkby to break away and score eleven times. John Abbey, G. Hunt, Brian Longbone and Victor Welburn were Dale's scorers.

13 JAN: SLINGSBY 7 DALE 1. Brian Longbone was the Dale marksman.

20 JAN: TERRINGTON 4 DALE 0.

27 JAN: AISLABY UNITED 7 DALE 1. Brian Longbone was at it again.

3 FEB: ROSEDALE 7 DALE 0.

24 FEB: BAGBY & BALK 6 DALE 1. John Abbey scored but Dale just lacked that finishing touch.

3 MAR: DALE 0 COXWOLD 4. Dale were playing well until Steve Hill went off with a gashed leg. You can hardly have expected Dale to have played well without Steve Hill, and they didn't. Mike Avison and Robin Cass were ok, though.

10 MAR: KIRKDALE UNITED 2 DALE 2. Dale ended their barren run in this Hospital Cup replay. Ashley White scored thanks to a deflection and John Abbey knocked in number two. Kirkdale scored two in the second half.

17 MAR: DALE 2 AMPLEFORTH 2. Ampleforth went ahead but on form John Abbey equalised. Again Ampleforth took the lead, and again Abbey equalised. Mike Avison performed heroics in goal.

24 MAR: KIRKDALE UNITED 2 DALE 5. They say anything can happen in the Cup, and it certainly did as Dale knocked in an incredible five goals to earn a lucrative trip to Hovingham. Brian Longbone grabbed a hat trick much to the delight of the huge travelling army.

31 MAR: HOVINGHAM 6 DALE 1. Dale's Cup run came to an abrupt end although they did have a weakened side. Michael Metcalfe was the scorer.

7 APR: DALE 1 DUNCOMBE PARK 2. After Dale went in at half time trailing 2-0, they hit back in the second half through never say die Victor Welburn.

14 APR: DALE 2 GILLAMOOR 6. Dale cruised into a slick two goal lead but, erm, Gillamoor replied with six more.

21 APR: DALE 5 FARNDALE 2. Steve Hill, Victor Welburn, John Abbey, Mike Metcalfe and Ashley White were the scorers as Dale went goals crazy.

28 APR: SINNINGTON 4 DALE 0. Apparently, Dale were determined and Les Welburn had a stunning game.

5 MAY: DALE 0 AISLABY UNITED 3. This week it was a sturdy display from Dale's youngsters.

Our complete record for the 1982/3 season:
Pld 30, won 5, drew 2, lost 23, goals for 51, goals against 160, points 12, position 13th out of 16.

****

1983/4

3 SEP: AMPLEFORTH 4 DALE 4. Ampleforth held a 3-1 interval lead, but Dale showed their legendary fighting qualities in coming back to share the points thanks to goals from Brian Longbone (2), Victor Welburn and Michael Metcalfe.

10 SEP: DALE 0 AISLABY UNITED 4.

17 SEP: AISLABY UNITED 8 DALE 0.

24 SEP: DALE 1 TERRINGTON 2. The visitors led 2-0 at half time. Robin Cass was replaced by super sub Ashley Welburn at the interval due to injury but although Brian Longbone hit the net, Terrington hung on for victory.

1 OCT: DALE 0 GILLAMOOR 1. Apparently Mike Avison had a good game for Dale.

8 OCT: DALE 3 BAGBY AND BALK 3. Victor Welburn was toast of the village after his last gasp equaliser salvaged a share of the points. Bagby went one up before Michael Metcalfe scored with a 20 yard netbuster. Again the visitors took the advantage going 3-1 ahead before Mike Downing reduced the arrears and Victor did the business.

15 OCT: HOVINGHAM 6 DALE 2. Ace marksman Brian Longbone was at it again, lashing home two stunners to give Dale a sensational lead. The home side grabbed a goal before the break and slotted home five more in the second half.

22 OCT: COXWOLD 10 DALE 0. Well, you can't win 'em all.

29 OCT: DALE 2 DUNCOMBE PARK 3. Brian Longbone and Michael Metcalfe scored for Dale, who still managed to lose by the odd goal in five. Robin Cass and Mike Avison were outstanding.

5 NOV: WESTLERS RESERVES 4 DALE 1. Dreams of Hospital Cup glory filled the Greyhound Ground as Richard Dawson shot Dale into a ninth minute lead. Sadly it was not to be as Westlers hit four, although Mike Avison saved a penalty in the second half.

12 NOV: DALE 2 KIRKDALE UNITED 2. Michael Metcalfe put Dale ahead and after the visitors had levelled the scores, hot shot Victor Welburn hit the home side back in front. Kirkdale equalised early in the second half.

19 NOV: DALE 0 SINNINGTON 4. Player/manager Ashley Welburn steered the ball into his own net to give Sinnington the lead. After two further strikes, Mike Downing rounded things off in style with a second Dale own goal.

26 NOV: DALE 4 FARNDALE 7. In those halycon days, Farndale were the Halifax of the Beckett League. Yet they still managed to record their biggest ever victory on a barmy winter afternoon at the Greyhound Ground. Robin Cass and Victor Welburn scored as Dale strolled into a 2-0 lead but they were soon shell-shocked as Farndale replied with seven! Robin Cass again and Steve Avison got the consolation goals.

10 DEC: DALE 2 KIRKBYMOORSIDE RESERVES 1. They were singing in The Buck that night as two Michael Metcalfe strikes earned brave Dale their first win of the season. Stand in keeper Robin Cass made a breathtaking save with seconds left to ensure victory.

17 DEC: SLINGSBY 2 DALE 2. After a goal-less first half, Brian Longbone shot Dale into the lead on 70 minutes. A minute later the home team equalised and soon afterwards went in front, but Victor Welburn did it again - a great equaliser with the last kick of the game from a Steve Avison corner.

31 DEC: DALE 2 SLINGSBY 7. Ever reliable Brian Longbone put Dale into the lead but the visitors replied - seven times. Robin Cass knocked in a consolation penalty late on.

7 JAN: ROSEDALE 4 DALE 3. Into 1984 with a seven goal thriller! Richard Dawson, Michael Metcalfe and Brian Longbone again hit the mark for Dale.

4 FEB: FARNDALE 4 DALE 2. After a long break due to bad weather Dale fell once more to the might of Farndale. After the home side went two ahead, Victor Welburn pulled a goal back and Ashley White equalised from a precise cross by Michael Metcalfe. Then we went to pieces and lost again.

11 FEB: TERRINGTON 3 DALE 2. Victor Welburn struck first in what was a thrilling and entertaining game. The home team went in at the interval 2-1 ahead thanks in part to a Mike Avison own goal. Michael Metcalfe equalised but Terrington scored again to leave Dale pointless.

18 FEB: KIRKBYMOORSIDE RESERVES 1 DALE 1. This one will go down in history! Apparently Dale went behind when keeper Derek Greenbank mishandled. But Greenbank became the Dale hero when he converted a last minute cross from Robin Cass to earn a draw! Bruce Grobbelaar eat your heart out! Les Welburn was outstanding for Dale.

25 FEB: The gallant lads of Coxwold football team couldn't make their Beckett League fixture at Thornton Dale on Saturday. Fire broke out at a nearby farm and they stayed back to fight it!

3 MAR: SINNINGTON 6 DALE 0.

7 MAR: KIRKDALE UNITED 3 DALE 2. Ashley White put Dale into the lead but Kirkdale soon equalised. Again White put Dale ahead, but again Kirkdale replied. Two minutes from the end of the game, Kirkdale hit the winner.

10 MAR: BAGBY AND BALK 3 DALE 0. Bagby took the lead and then Dale suffered a blow when Keith Holmes went off injured, leaving them with just ten men. The brave lads held on for a respectable three goal defeat.

17 MAR: DALE 1 AMPLEFORTH 6. After a goal-less first half, Ampleforth took the initiative and found the net six times. Ian Holmes grabbed a consolation goal for never-say-die Dale.

24 MAR: DUNCOMBE PARK 13 DALE 0. A brief hiccup from the lads there.

31 MAR: DALE 1 HOVINGHAM 3. Aiming to make amends for the previous week's disaster, Dale started well and after Michael Metcalfe had clipped the crossbar, Victor Welburn lashed the ball home, only for it to be disallowed for offside. Robin Cass then scored a brilliant solo goal but the visitors rode the early storm and got the points.

14 APR: DALE 3 ROSEDALE 6. Rosedale's second double of the season.

21 APR: GILLAMOOR 1 DALE 0.

28 APR: DALE 0 COXWOLD 7. Bloody Coxwold again.

****

1984/5

1 SEP: TERRINGTON 7 DALE 0.

3 SEP: DALE 2 AYTON RESERVES 3. Dawson and Avison did the business.

8 SEP: DALE 4 ROSEDALE 4. Richard Thorner, Andy Hill, Steve Avison and Richard Dawson scored as Dale snatched a point.

11 SEP: DALE 0 TERRINGTON 4.

15 SEP: SINNINGTON 5 DALE 1. Nigel Aconley got the consolation goal.

22 SEP: BAGBY & BALK 7 DALE 1. Bagby hit six in the second half despite a goal from the reliable Andy Hill.

29 SEP: AYTON RESERVES 1 DALE 2. Fresh faced sixteen year old Billy Balderson equalised and Richard Thorner coolly slotted home a penalty for Dale's first victory of the campaign. All three goals came in a torrid first half. Eddie Avison and Robin Cass were outstanding in defence.

6 OCT: ROSEDALE 9 DALE 2. Dale used up all their energy in the first half, going in equal at 2-2 courtesy of Richard Dawson and Ashley White. Rosedale stepped up a few gears after the break and left Dale for dead.

13 OCT: DALE 1 WESTLERS RESERVES 7. Another second half disaster here as Dale went in at half time level, Steve Avison getting the goal this week.

20 OCT: SLINGSBY 6 DALE 1. Robin Cass scored, and the wayward Richard Thorner missed a penalty.

27 OCT: KIRKBYMOORSIDE RESERVES 2 DALE 1. After a goalless first half, Steve Avison put Dale in front but that famous collapse was just around the corner. Kenny Hill had an impressive debut, though.

NOV 3: DALE 1 COXWOLD 9. Here we go again. Dale were one up at half time, did bugger all in the second half and Coxwold scored nine consolation goals.

NOV 17: AISLABY UNITED 5 DALE 0.

DEC 6: DALE 0 TERRINGTON 1.

DEC 8: FARNDALE 5 DALE 3. Ashley White, Kenny Hill and Own Goal scored for Dale.

DEC 15: DALE 0 BAGBY & BALK 7.

DEC 28: KIRKDALE UNITED 3 DALE 4. A real Christmas cracker, this one. Steve Avison and Ashley White scored early on, then Andy Hill grabbed the winner with five minutes remaining. That defensive stalwart Robin Cass impressed again.

10 JAN: WESTLERS RESERVES 4 DALE 2. Steve Avison scored first after tireless work from Kenny Hill. Westlers went ahead but Andy Hill equalised. The home team then stepped up a gear and won easily.

2 FEB: DALE 6 KIRKDALE 0. Steve Avison went goals crazy, slamming in four while the other scorers were Andy Hill and Richard Thorner.

9 FEB: DALE v AISLABY UNITED. The game was abandoned after 22 minutes because the pitch was unplayable. Aislaby led 2-0 at the time!

16 FEB: DALE 3 AMPLEFORTH 2. Steve Avison and Ashley Welburn scored for Dale and it looked like a draw until Andy Hill scored the winner with seven minutes remaining. Colin Hogg had a fine game for Dale.

23 FEB: GILLAMOOR 3 DALE 3. Andy Hill scored twice and David Hodgson rescued a point with a beauty into the top corner of the net.

2 MAR: AMPLEFORTH 4 DALE 3. Dale had gone into a two goal lead thanks to dynamic brothers Andy and Kenny Hill. Ampleforth hit three but David Hodgson equalised. The home team got an undeserved last minute winner.
9 MAR: DALE 0 AISLABY UNITED 3.

23 MAR: DALE 1 DUNCOMBE PARK 10. Dale's leaky defence were at it again.

30 MAR: DALE 6 FARNDALE 2. It was hat-ricks galore at the Greyhound Ground as Robin Cass and Andy Hill knocked in three each. Kenny Hill had another great game.

6 APR: DALE 1 SINNINGTON 3. Dale only had 10 men in the second half after referee Derek Greenbank sent a player off. Ashley White scored to round off a brave Dale display.

10 APR: DALE 1 SLINGSBY 6. Colin Hogg scored for Dale but Slingsby improved as the game went on.

13 APR: DALE 3 GILLAMOOR 2. Kenny Hill grabbed another Dale hat-rick in the first hour. Gillamoor came back strongly but Dale just hung on.

17 APR: COXWOLD 3 DALE 4. Lowly Dale stunned the Beckett League with a great victory. Andy Hill scored twice and could even afford to miss a penalty. Coxwold led 3-2 but Hill got the customary Dale hat-rick and Ashley Welburn finished things off in style after a good pass from young starlet Richard Thorner.

20 APR: DALE 6 KIRKBYMOORSIDE RESERVES 0. On a rainy afternoon Dale rounded off the season on a high note. The visiting keeper wasn't very pleased and hurled obscenity after obscenity at the amused Dale fans behind the goal.

****

1985/6

7 SEP: AISLABY UNITED 1 DALE 1. Brian Longbone scored a controversial goal for Dale.

14 SEP: COXWOLD 4 DALE 1. Richard Dawson scored for Dale.

18 SEP: Dale travelled to Ayton Reserves and won. God knows what the score was, though.

21 SEP: DUNCOMBE PARK 22 (yes, 22) DALE 0. A bit of a dodgy performance from our back four there.

28 SEP: DALE 1 FARNDALE 3. Andy Hill got the goal.

5 OCT: AMPLEFORTH 11 DALE 0. Well, it was a bit better than our previous away trip.

12 OCT: DALE 0 WESTLERS RESERVES 24 (yes, 24). The stuff memories are made of. A 24 goal thriller.

19 OCT: ROSEDALE 10 DALE 0. Dale battled well in a sporting game.

A week later, Thornton Dale Reserves FC resigned from the Beckett League. They would never grace the Greyhound Ground turf again. It was the end of a golden era. The end of a football legend...

www.ingramcontent.com/pod-product-compliance
Lightning Source LLC
Chambersburg PA
CBHW081047180526
45170CB00005B/1724